TEST
AND
PROTEST

TEST
AND
RETEST

TEST AND PROTEST

The Influence of Consumers Union

Norman Isaac Silber

HOLMES & MEIER
New York   London

First published in the United States of America 1983 by
Holmes & Meier Publishers, Inc.
30 Irving Place
New York, N.Y. 10003

Great Britain:
Holmes & Meier Publishers, Ltd.
131 Trafalgar Road
Greenwich, London SE10 9TX

Book design by Rose Jacobowitz

Library of Congress Cataloging in Publication Data
Silber, Norman Isaac.
    Test and protest.

    Includes bibliographical references and index.
    1. Consumer education—United States—History.
2. Consumer protection—United States—History.
3. Consumers Union of United States.   I. Title.
TX335.S553   1983   363.1'057   83-6179
ISBN 0-8419-0749-8 (cl)
ISBN 0-8419-0877-x

Manufactured in the United States of America

To the memory of
Max and Dracia Silber

About the Author

Norman I. Silber has taught at Yale and Sarah Lawrence colleges. Born in 1951, he grew up in Skokie, Illinois, graduated summa cum laude from Washington University in Saint Louis, and received a Ph.D. from Yale University in 1978. An interviewer for the Columbia University Oral History Project, Mr. Silber served as the historian for a National Endowment for the Humanities project which established an archive for consumer history. He is a member of several consumer organizations. Mr. Silber lives with his wife, Nancy, in New York.

Contents

Acknowledgments

THIS WORK BENEFITED from the interest shown by many people. I am grateful to John Morton Blum for refining my prose and sustaining my involvement. The late Arthur Leff was a perceptive adviser and an inspiring teacher. David Brion Davis offered valuable criticism. The willingness of Colston Warne to share his extraordinary experiences led me to understand better the consumer movement and its leaders.

Marie Caskey, Steven Mintz, Patricia Nelson, Robert Post, Robert Cover, and Alex Aleinikoff debated problems with me and made suggestions that improved the manuscript. I want to thank people who listened to my views and helped in other ways: Nathan Laks, Jeff Limerick, Joyce Newman Marcus, Geoffrey Miller, Rachelle and Shaul Mishal, David Pollard, Robert Everett, Cathy and George Shockey, Jack Silber, Jeffrey Silber, and Florence Thomas. I learned from students in my seminars at Yale and Sarah Lawrence colleges. Margaret Hainer, Harold Field, and Aya Betensky edited the manuscript with sensitivity. Eugene and Elizabeth Aleinikoff encouraged me to see this through to publication. Without Nancy Aleinikoff Silber, this could not have been as fulfilling a project or as happy an undertaking. For errors and omissions I have only myself to thank.

Preface

IN JANUARY 1977, Colston E. Warne, a tall, soft-spoken, seventy-eight-year-old economist, presented the first of eight lectures about the origins of consumerism to an audience at Kansas State University. At the heart of his narrative was Consumers Union of United States, an organization that Warne had helped to lead as its president for nearly all of the previous forty-one years. "In telling this story," Warne began, "I fully recognize the difficulty of being objective. . . . Nevertheless, as the last surviving member of the original board of CU, I will do my best to maintain the objectivity which has been characteristic of CU since its inception." Warne went on to discuss the nature of the American marketplace, the history of consumer protest, and the growth of the international consumer movement. Three months later, when he finished his series, Warne had honored his original intentions; he had delivered a series of talks that were scholarly and objective, and yet strongly conveyed the message of an advocate for the consumer movement.

My study began as an exploration of themes that Warne had addressed: a consideration of the history of selected American consumer problems. As this research continued, however, it became clear that in addition to pioneering in the consumer movement, Consumers Union (CU), founded in 1936, was among the earliest and most durable organizations in the history of American reform to bring scientists, journalists, and social activists together in one venture. "The idea of testing and appraising products by name," Warne maintained, "constituted an overdue scientific mechanism designed to restore rationality to the marketplace." This idea, he had written earlier, amounted to nothing less than a social invention.

The realization that scientific testing for the purpose of consumer reform was a twentieth-century phenomenon provoked several questions. Why did the techniques of objective science become useful to consumer activists when they did? Were these techniques in conflict with older

modes of persuasion used by different reformers, or were they com-
plementary? How did a commitment to science modify a commitment to
social change? It became apparent that a study of product testing at CU
might answer these questions and illuminate the developing ways that
reformers appropriated the logic of science and relied on popular faith in
scientific evidence to promote their own vision of social progress.

The case studies that were chosen as the most promising for this
investigation were the reform of automotive design, the discouragement
of smoking, and the prevention of the contamination of food by radioactive fallout. These chapters in the history of environmental health and
public safety were selected because of the part Consumers Union played
in them, because of their centrality to contemporary concerns, and because of their continuing importance to consumer and environmental
studies. The product testing discussed here would rank high on a list of
the most ambitious projects undertaken by Consumers Union, but the
discussion is not intended to be a complete picture of the activities of that
organization.*

An understanding of the path taken by Consumers Union requires a
preliminary look at the traditional themes of consumer protest and a view
of the historical development of consumer product testing. The case
studies and conclusions which follow describe the dilemmas, difficulties,
and successes that resulted from the attempt to be objective, scientific,
and yet committed to a vision of reform at one and the same time.

New York City   *1983*

TEST
AND
PROTEST

CHAPTER I

The Tradition of Consumer Protest

THE ACT OF BEING a consumer, one American consumer advocate explained, "is so common and so inescapable that, like the air around us, we mostly take it for granted." The routine necessity of consumption and the many problems that surround it have led to many different views of the consumer interest, and to many kinds of consumer protest. At first, opposition to unsatisfactory goods and the ways they were obtained developed locally, and the remedies for consumer problems rested with individual buyers and sellers. Late in nineteenth-century America, a national culture of consumption emerged; national movements of consumers organized at the same time. At every level of size and intensity, the voices of consumer discontent addressed three main issues: the unreliability of sellers; the scarcity, social distortion, and high prices created by insufficient production; and the need to incorporate ethical considerations into the decisions made in the marketplace.[1]

The Unreliability of Sellers

Efforts to prevent losses, injuries, and inconveniences resulting from deceptive and irregular selling practices began early in the history of commercial societies. Roman emperors tried to govern trading practices in their grain markets. Medieval guild regulations protected the reputation of craftsmen by establishing standards for quality and rules for the display of wares. Sixteenth- and seventeenth-century biblical commentary delineated codes for ethical behavior in the marketplace. Punishments for adulterating, contaminating, and shortweighting food supplies were meted out often in eighteenth-century Europe and colonial North

1

America. Napoleonic health councils regulated the nutritional quality of bread and devised toxicological tests to determine the purity of wine and medicine. With varying degrees of success and awareness, consumers, producers, and market authorities tried to establish equitable rules and minimum standards of truth and safety in order to encourage trade.[2]

Economic growth and unsettling social change in the United States during the nineteenth century made the traditional difficulties of intelligent consumer choice more acute. Trying to make consumption appropriate and efficient, Lydia Maria Child, Catherine Beecher, and Harriet Beecher Stowe wrote treatises about household science that examined problems including the changing nature of food preparation, the growing preoccupation with cleanliness inside the house, and the increasing dependence of families on store-bought goods. As the chief buyers for the family, women realized the importance of conserving their time, effort, and health by bringing regularity and routine to housework. The absence of routine, according to Beecher, meant that "instead of being the intelligent regulators of their own time," women had become "the mere sport of circumstance." The regularization of the household entailed simplification of tasks, knowledge about the true value of goods, and greater control by consumers over the goods that were bought.[3]

The problem of regularizing consumption also became important for companies that needed to purchase raw materials of uniform quality in great quantities for their growing volume of production. Purchasing agents for munitions, refining, locomotive, bicycle, food preparation, and other businesses developed techniques for sampling raw materials and for buying according to contracted specifications. Companies established small laboratories for the purpose of improving the oversight of raw materials that they received. Certain businesses specialized in helping other firms to regularize their consumption. Arthur D. Little, an independent chemist, expanded his laboratory into a testing agency in 1886. An association of insurance underwriters received a charter in 1901 to label different brands of wire and lighting fixtures as fire-resistant in order to help electrical companies to construct insurable buildings. "The label is a certificate of character awarded to an inanimate object," an official history of Underwriters Laboratories (UL) observed. "It is an epitome of the technical skill, costly equipment, wide experience and thorough-going investigation that have been concentrated upon that object in the process of searching out its every point of weakness." Encouraged by the work of Frederick Taylor and the movement for scientific management, corporate efforts to improve the efficiency of production and purchasing spread after the turn of the century.[4]

The federal government, too, began to acknowledge the importance of bringing uniformity and predictability to its purchases. By 1906, the National Bureau of Standards was testing the quality of goods bought by the government and helping to formulate specifications for the goods that different agencies wanted to buy. In addition to setting minimum standards, the bureau used a grading system to distinguish varying degrees of quality. The bureau helped businesses to standardize their commercial weights and measures, educated industrial buyers about measuring and testing apparatuses, and informed them of ways to control quality. "Scarcely a day passes that some manufacturer does not visit the Bureau to learn how to measure or secure standards," remarked its director.[5]

While businesses and the government during the early years of the century increasingly purchased according to standards and specifications, consumers of finished products did not find those techniques available. Consumers instead found a profusion of unstandardized packaged goods, cans, boxes, and cartons. New, unfamiliar selling and processing techniques outmoded many timeworn methods of judging, for example, the freshness of food or the durability of clothing.[6]

To ease the minds of customers about problems of quality, reliability, and safety, manufacturers and advertisers appealed to consumers to buy according to brand name. National Biscuit, Heinz Soup, Armour Meat, Standard Oil, and other companies placed one banner on many different products. The consumer who found one product of a brand to be satisfactory, those companies suggested, could assume that all other products also would be suitable. Popular magazines offered to help readers with the selection of goods, and women's magazines, particularly, issued advice about the correct way to evaluate new products. In 1902, *Good Housekeeping* developed a "Seal of Approval" which it hoped would become a symbol of reputability. *Good Housekeeping* authorized placement of the seal on goods it judged worthy of advertising space in its pages; in effect, it placed its brand on the other brands. For American consumers, the search for a brand one could trust was the chief way to make buying more convenient and secure.[7]

The public soon learned to be skeptical of even the most respected of the advertised brands. Demonstrating the tangible, pervasive corruption of major trusts and corporations, Upton Sinclair, Lincoln Steffens, Ida Tarbell, Samuel Hopkins Adams, Mark Sullivan, and other muckrakers found the public deeply interested in issues of adulteration and deception. Sinclair especially, with his vivid descriptions of putrid meat, watered milk, and doctored dry goods, "hit the public's stomach" with *The Jungle* (1906), and helped to mobilize popular outrage about the conditions of the sale and manufacture of meat. Supported by the muckrakers, women's groups, business interests, and others, Dr. Harvey

1.1 *Good Housekeeping* magazine developed a Roll of
Honor for Pure Food Products, with the help of Dr.
Harvey Wiley, in December 1905. *Good Housekeeping*
awarded the five-point star to products that it approved.
Reproduced with permission from the Hearst Corpora-
tion, publishers of *Good Housekeeping*.

Wiley, chief chemist at the Department of Agriculture, shepherded the
first Pure Food and Drug Law through Congress in 1906.[8]
    The passage of food and drug regulation marked one step toward
more efficient consumption. According to an article written in 1912 by
Wesley Clair Mitchell, however, the fundamental reason for "The Backward Art of Spending Money" was the persistence of the household as the
basic buying unit in American life. Innovations in productive techniques
apparently had improved industrial efficiency, but factors including love,
parental affection, and racial ties cemented families together and ensured
that consumption would remain inefficiently atomistic, "standardized in
the institution of monogamy." Mitchell called for a national commitment
to the establishment of a science of household consumption.[9]
    Concerted efforts to develop such a helping profession of consumer
scientists intensified, particularly among women. The activities of Ellen
Swallow Richards and others, which led to the creation of the American
Home Economics Association in 1908; the educational work of the federal
Bureau of Home Economics and the Cooperative Extension Services; the

popularity of the Country Life and Public Health movements; and the introduction of consumer education and home economics courses in colleges all indicated a regard for promoting a higher level of knowledge about efficiency, thrift, and safety in purchasing. In spite of those voluntary educational and professional activities, the problems persisted. Consumers had not time, information, or equipment to "candle every egg . . . test the milk . . . inquire into the shoddy [or] find out whether the newspapers are lying," as Walter Lippmann wrote in 1914. The problem, in the view of Lippmann and others, resided less in the failure to educate consumers than in the failure to coordinate and control producers.[10]

The attempt to improve consumption by rationalizing production made remarkable gains during the First World War. Prodded by the War Industries Board to conserve resources and to meet government specifications, producers stabilized the quality of their products and reduced the number of styles, varieties, sizes, and colors that they offered:

> The clothing industry was revolutionized from the skin out . . .
> shoe lasts were reduced in number and shoe colors restricted to
> black, white and one shade of tan. . . . Colors of typewriter
> ribbons shrank from 150 to 5 and were sold in heavy paper
> instead of tinfoil. . . . Buggy wheels were reduced from 232 sizes
> and varieties to 4, plows from 326 to 76 sizes and styles, and
> automobile tires from 287 types to 9.

The Conservation Division of the Council of National Defense estimated that savings on the home front were achieved in 250 industries.[11]

The necessities of war encouraged standardization, but the 1920s brought a debate about the value of its further extension. Various labor leaders and businessmen argued that together with scientific management techniques, the imposition of standards hastened the regimentation of life and led to the sacrifice of diversity, choice, and individuality for the sake of uniformity and predictability. Opponents of the large trusts feared that the standardization of goods might foster monopoly, reduce the rate of technological change, and ultimately lead to higher prices for consumer goods.[12]

To other engineers and businessmen, intermediate standardization represented a liberating element. According to Albert Whitney of the insurance industry, the adherence to standards permitted the technological equivalent of a process of natural selection. In the tradition of Herbert Spencer, Whitney believed that in nature, there were two fundamentally divergent tendencies—"a force that is continually operating to produce greater variety, and . . . a force that is continually operating to eliminate

unsuccessful variations and to concentrate upon . . . [a] few types which
. . . are reproduced faithfully from generation to generation." Standardization helped society "to capitalize an advance by making it a prevailing
type." Any loss of individuality or aesthetic value due to standards, Frederick Schlink and Robert Brady concurred, was the result "not of conscious efforts to achieve economy and wide distribution of goods, but of
competitive businesslike efforts put forth in the interest of increasing
profits, or the omnipresent human tendency to do whatever others are
doing in considerable numbers."[13]

Efforts to document the waste that resulted from the absence of
standards uncovered dramatic examples of unnecessary and costly irregu-
larities in practices of production. According to the American Standards
Association (formed in 1919), American firms lost millions of dollars in
contracts with British companies because tolerances for screw and bolt
threads were not uniform. A careful survey of waste in industry by Secretary of Commerce Herbert Hoover in 1921 led him to estimate that
practically half of the material, labor, energy, and human effort spent by
American manufacturing was "without tangible return." Encouraged by
Hoover, the Bureau of Standards, and the American Standards Association, firms by the hundreds during the 1920s adopted standards and
specifications.[14]

Equating waste with inefficiency, the perspective of Hoover and
most industrialists focused on the financial losses that resulted from
waste. But Thorstein Veblen defined the problem in broader terms. Between 1899 and 1923, Veblen developed an institutional analysis of irra-
tionality throughout society. Man, in his argument, was by heredity
inclined to value commodities that were useful and workmanlike, but a
cultural tendency on the part of the leisure class to maintain social standing by "conspicuous consumption" overpowered that instinct. Through a
process of "emulation," the "pecuniary canons of taste" of the leisure class
permeated all of American culture and deeply affected aesthetic and
moral values. Wastefulness was the result—a quality that Veblen attached
to every expenditure that did not "serve human life or human well-being
on the whole." Even though an expenditure was not wasteful "as viewed
from the standpoint of the individual consumer who chooses it," it was
wasteful from the standpoint of social welfare. "In order to meet with
unqualified approval," Veblen wrote, "any economic fact must approve
itself under the test of impersonal usefulness—usefulness as seen from
the point of view of the generically human." Veblen deflated the "captain
of industry" and hoped for a new industrial order based on the competence and independence of the engineer. In effect, he shared the enthusiasm of several earlier utilitarian socialists, particularly Edward

Bellamy, for a world where the desirability of goods was proportional to their functional value. Veblen wanted to replace the judgments of individual consumers, or the choices induced by advertising, with the engineer's standard of usefulness.[15]

Stuart Chase accepted and gave additional meaning to Veblen's conception of waste. An accountant by profession and a member with Veblen of Howard Scott's short-lived Technocratic movement of the early 1930s, Chase believed that the experience of planning, testing, and standardizing during World War I supported his faith that the federal government and industry could work toward positive social goals. The simple elimination of inefficiency for Chase was only "another method of increasing profit under the price system." The efficiency drive, he wrote, could serve either "social or anti-social ends"—it could contribute to waste or else help to eliminate it. In *The Challenge of Waste* (1922) and later in *The Tragedy of Waste* (1925), Chase drew attention to a flood of products that were "seriously detrimental to man and quite outside the category of wants," including hundreds of items:

> many patent medicines, distilled spirits, opium, machine guns, poison gas, prostitution, gambling and speculation, quackery, super-luxuries, dishonest advertising . . . and all else that breaks or distorts the minds of men.

A less dangerous class of goods, including chewing gum, much advertising, fashions, moving pictures, tobacco, and best-sellers, did "no particular good and no particular harm to the consumer of them." Together, the detrimental and questionable goods amounted to the opposite of wealth, or "illth," a term adapted from the English writer John Ruskin. Because of that waste, the great majority of Americans lived below a minimum budget of health and decency. When society through complacency or intention fostered destructive or wasteful habits, "the labor power of a large number of people was diverted from the production of goods to the production of ills." By the mid 1920s, the problem of inefficiency—and of waste in that broader sense—had become a central theme of consumer protest.[16]

Scarcity

Nineteenth-century classical economic theory suggested that in a state of perfect competition, the strength of consumer demand determined the success or failure of a product. The genuine needs of consumers were determined rationally and then satisfied to the greatest possible extent. But as Adam Smith observed in *The Wealth of Nations* (1776), consumer demand frequently stood captive to the variables of production. Although "the sole end and purpose of all production is consumption," Smith wrote, "the interest of the consumer is almost constantly sacrificed to that of the producer." A century later, Simon Patten, an economist at the University of Pennsylvania, observed that, at the least, the relative capabilities of technology restricted the freedom of choice of consumers. "We produce to consume . . . but what we will desire to consume is largely determined by the cost of production," Patten noted.[17]

The paradox of consumption controlled by producers or by the technology of production became more evident with the increasing complexity and size of the productive and distributive process. "Few consumers feel any of that sense of power which economists say is theirs," Walter Lippmann wrote in 1914. The consumer "takes what he can get at the price he can afford. He is told what he wants, and then he wants it. He rides in a packed subway because he has to, and he buys a certain kind of soap because it has been thrust upon his soul. Where there is a monopoly the consumer is, of course, helpless, and where there is competition he is at the mercy of advertising." The picture of demand-stimulated production painted by most classical economists amounted "to a crass abstraction, industrialism idealized until it is no longer industrialism."[18]

Mass production required mass consumption, and the role of advertising expanded to replace the face-to-face contact between buyer and seller of earlier days. Prior to the First World War, the need to increase production appeared to be the greatest challenge to national prosperity. At the end of the war and for most of the two decades that followed, manufacturers of many basic and secondary products confronted problems of overproduction and consumer resistance to new products. To increase the volume of sales of products, individual firms and trade associations turned to advertising agents to find ways to "engineer" a demand for goods, to legitimize obsolescence, and to capture larger shares of the consumer's dollar. "Consumption engineering," declared Ernest Elmo Calkins, a well-respected advertising agent, "does not end until we can consume all we make."[19]

To accelerate the rate at which Americans spent their money, advertisers carried new levels of sophistication to their work. Promising beautiful feet when they sold stockings and adventure when they sold automobiles, they began to master the soft sell. They developed giveaway prizes, celebrity testimonials, slogans, jingles, and graphic emblems. In 1923 Veblen reported his view that the process of creating demand had become dependable and mechanistic. "The fabrication of customers," he

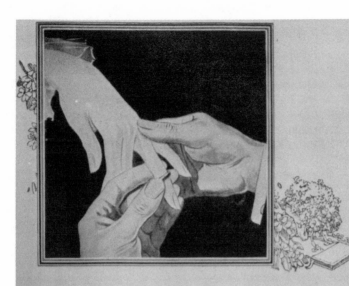

Keep that hand soft!

"We can't afford servants," said most young married couples fifty years ago. "They cost too much in wages and food."

But there is no bride today who cannot afford the *modern* servants—the electric devices that ask for no afternoon off, eat nothing, and work untiringly for an average wage of 3 cents an hour.

GENERAL ELECTRIC

1.2 During the 1920s, advertisements for vacuum cleaners, irons, and other appliances emphasized the therapeutic value of higher standards of cleanliness and the desirability of appearing not to have done housework. Advertisement for General Electric reproduced with permission from *Life*, June 14, 1923.

wrote, "can now be carried on as a routine operation, quite in the spirit of the mechanical industries and with much the same degree of assurance as regards the quality, rate and volume of the output." The advertising industry, in contrast, conceived of its task in more creative and less predictable terms. "We who have to bring in business, must get out before the customer and shout, search, halloo, promise, concede, coax, be funny, coo, thump, seek, knock, punch and *get* the order," advertised one New York agency. Regardless of the state of development of the art of selling, few economists of the time denied the importance of advertising to the financial viability of techniques of mass production.[20]

Advertising during the 1920s increasingly appealed to Americans to use up what they bought and to be satisfied only with the newest and best. "By making the luxuries of today the necessities of tomorrow," the publicity director of Shredded Wheat declared, "advertising creates prosperity, alters social beliefs, and advances civilization." That view at first seemed shocking to many, particularly after wartime thrift campaigns. But adjustment to extravagance as a "virtue" came rapidly.[21]

Wealth accumulated and aggregate consumption spiraled rapidly upward during the 1920s. National income (adjusted in constant dollars) grew by more than 40 percent per capita between 1909 and 1929. Accumulating close to four billion dollars in short-term debts in 1929 alone, American families sharply increased their use of credit. Robert Lynd, the author of *Middletown* (1925) and a member of the Hoover Commission on Recent Social Trends, observed that consumers had entered a new culture of possessiveness. Cars and telephones had become commonplace. New trends in construction had changed the house from "a simple box with holes for doors and light" to a more complicated structure. The broom, "unchanged since the Egyptians," had given way to the vacuum cleaner. The habit of taking a vacation was spreading. These material changes had come together with a more basic shift in social values:

> The increasing secularization of spending and the general pleasure basis of living . . . the new gospel which encourages liberal spending to make the wheels of industry turn as a duty of the citizen . . . the new attitude toward hardship as a thing to be avoided by living in the here and now, utilizing credit and other devices to telescope the future into the present . . . making money in order to buy a living . . .

Before the twenties had ended, many people had adjusted to a life-style of "consuming," or using up what they bought, and wanting more.[22]

The onset of the Depression did not mark the beginning of cynicism toward advertising, but it did magnify and popularize apprehension and distrust that intellectuals harbored toward the culture of salesmanship and business. Whether material possessions had brought happiness during the 1920s, millions after 1929 were devastated by their sudden inability to provide for the future or to keep what they owned. It was not possible to isolate the hollow feeling of being without work from the deprivation and torment born out of the inability to consume. For millions of people—especially those women and the elderly who did not ordinarily get paid for their labor—it was not unemployment but the psychology of compulsory consumer restraint and the absence of disposable income that posed the chief hardship of the Depression.[23]

Resentment at a declining standard of living was especially great in the face of underutilized productive capacity. Veblen received relatively little public notice when, in *The Engineers and the Price System* (1919), he asserted that modern industry sabotaged production by adjusting "the rate and volume of output to the needs of the market, not to the working capacity of available resources, . . . nor to the community's need of consumable goods." In the years after the crash, however, the public became more receptive to the idea that scarcity was being managed. In spite of widespread demand for consumer goods, the quality of goods deteriorated and production collapsed for the lack only of a profitable market. From Technocracy to Townsendism, utopian proposals to establish minimum standards of living or unbounded production flourished.[24]

As advertisers continued to appeal to a higher standard of living than most Americans could afford, popular criticism of "artificially" created demand became bitter. The *Michigan Alumnus* reported that "without the help of Amos and Andy, or the personal endorsement of motion picture stars," Michigan students were flocking to "Depression Toothpaste," a mixture of salt and baking soda. "Today, for every shooting box containing an advertising man devising a new sales stimulus for Camels," wrote E. B. White, "there is a breadline full of men who know, without being told, just how badly they want a cigarette." Colston Warne, a young economist at Amherst with experience in the labor and cooperative movements, explained that "superlative claims are, like stocks, running today [1936] at a considerable discount from the New Era high. Appeals that you need this and that fall flat before an empty pocketbook, and out of despair comes a recognition that these 'great directing minds' of business are not so interested in consumer well-being as their pretenses would suggest." The perception of unaffordable goods, manipulated demand, and shattered expectations brought scarcity into focus as a second theme of protest.[25]

Ethical Consumption

A third category of consumer dissent developed not to express the dis-satisfaction of buyers, but to define their ethical responsibilities and to direct their economic power through boycotts. American revolutionaries had encouraged colonists to protest taxation by boycotting tea or news-papers. Nineteenth-century abolitionists tried to turn consumers against the products of slave labor. Civil rights activists in the 1960s would urge shoppers to boycott segregated stores and restaurants. Activists like these believed that the amoral character of economic exchange divorced con-siderations of social or political justice from routine decisions to buy and sell. A more extreme position held that the process of competitive enter-prise was essentially irreconcilable with higher social values. "Buying and selling is essentially anti-social in all its tendencies," Edward Bellamy wrote in *Looking Backward* (1887). "It is an education in self-seeking at the expense of others, and no society whose citizens are trained in such a school can possibly rise above a very low grade of civilization."[26]

A sense of obligation to the struggle of workers in fact motivated the first American consumer groups, the consumer clubs of the National Consumers' League. Created in 1891 to secure better working conditions for female clerks in department stores, the clubs published "white lists" of acceptable stores and refused to patronize others. Father John Elliot Ross of Catholic University in 1912 explained the view of the league that "the consuming class, in buying goods made under unjust terms, cooperate in injustice by receiving the goods, by furnishing the means for committing the injustice, and by urging such production by practical financial sup-port." Members of the league achieved notable successes in their efforts to "enlighten" and "organize" the "careless, money-spending public," and labor unions thereafter often tried to strengthen their economic power by organizing consumer boycotts.[27]

In cooperation with labor unions, the work of the National Consum-ers' League continued throughout the 1920s. Other groups, including prohibitionists, feminists, farmers, and religious fundamentalists, tried to make use of consumer boycotts as well. During the 1930s and 1940s, several effective boycotts were directed at fascism—"refusal to buy" movements aimed at products of Germany, Japan, and Falangist Spain.[28]

Many cooperative advocates during the Depression contended that if consumers applied sufficient pressure, a socialist commonwealth might emerge through a gradual transfer of ownership from capitalists to the state. Along lines encouraged by the English Fabians Beatrice and Syd-ney Webb, Americans including Seba Eldridge, Bertram Fowler, and E. J. Lever suggested that communal purchasing and selective boycotting

1.3 Advertisements for mouthwash during the Depression endeavored to build sales by exploiting worries about job security, which provoked resentment among consumer activists. Advertisement for Listerine reproduced with permission from *Life*, September 1934.

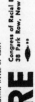
1.4   Two examples of ethical appeals to consumer interests. Appealing to the social responsibilities of consumers, activists in the civil rights movement during the early 1960s urged northerners to boycott companies whose Southern outlets refused integration at lunch counters; the labor movement also urged consumers to look beyond questions of quality and price to the conditions under which goods were produced. Both handbills reproduced courtesy of The New York Public Library, Astor, Lenox and Tilden Foundations, the Congress of Racial Equality, and the Amalgamated Clothing and Textile Workers Union.

could direct consumption in ethically more responsible ways. Services and utilities, including postal delivery, water supplies, and education, once had been run privately, Eldridge noted, but had become communal because people, in their capacities as purchasers, not as workers, were dissatisfied with private enterprise. "A citizen votes but once a year," observed Harold Loeb, a part of the Technocratic movement in 1932. "He buys commodities every day."[29]

Most New Deal politicians and intellectuals believed neither in the inherent barbarity of a market economy nor in the likelihood that organized consumer groups would form the vanguard of social revolution. "Who is a consumer? Show me a consumer," demanded General Hugh Johnson, head of Roosevelt's National Recovery Administration. John Chamberlain, then a radical journalist and the author of *Farewell to Reform* (1933), denied that it was possible to "get the victims of capitalist depression to organize as consumers." "People tend irrevocably to create their characters by reference to aptitudes which are bound up with the productive machine," he contended.[30]

But those persuaded of a growing consumer movement insisted that people soon would come to identify with their consuming functions. Arthur Feiler of the New School for Social Research conceded the tendency of people to associate "who they were" with "what they did for a living," but he saw nothing immutable about that fact. Horace Kallen, a fervent advocate of Christian cooperation, contended that habits of consumption would come to dominate the social identities of men because people were "consumers by nature, producers by necessity." According to Frederick Schlink, a founder of Consumers' Research, Inc., "producer consciousness" had developed only because people were "over-burdened" with the need to be productive:

> If [man] could get it into his head that [productive] activity is three-quarters waste because of bad social and economic organization, we would soon see him shift very quickly to primary interest in what he got for his expenditures.

In an economy of abundance where leisure was fostered by efficient production, or in a depression where it became difficult for consumers to make ends meet, the threads of consumer discontent might merge to create an alliance of consumers that contained meaning and importance.[31]

CHAPTER II

Consumer Reform
As a Science

IN 1927 FREDERICK SCHLINK AND Stuart Chase wrote *Your Money's Worth*, a story of "Alice in Wonderland, the consumer as Alice, modern salesmanship as wonderland." *Your Money's Worth* made a plea for the purchasing of consumer goods according to specifications, standards, and tests. It analyzed the ways Americans decided what they desired or needed, and asked how often goods delivered what their advertisers had promised. Chase and Schlink observed that the government had developed 11,000 specifications, "covering foodstuffs, soaps, metal polishes, hooks and eyes, motorboat engines . . . and so on indefinitely." Private industry had developed thousands of specifications. In contrast, the way goods were sold through normal channels of advertising relied more on fantasy and fiction than on careful attention to factual detail. "It is a maxim among advertising agents," they wrote, "that when you know the truth about anything, the real inner truth—it is very hard to write the surface stuff which sells it."[1]

The authors pleaded for an "extension of the principle of buying goods according to impartial scientific tests rather than according to the fanfare and trumpets of the higher salesmanship." Such a system would eliminate the need for most advertising, reduce costs, simplify the manufacturing process, clarify the determination of real consumer desires, and solve the problems of deliberate adulteration. "If the run of goods were as dependable as the [government-tested] fire truck on Main Street," they wrote, "Wonderland would well-nigh cease to be."

Consumers' Research

Within months, *Your Money's Worth* became a Book-of-the-Month best seller. Hundreds of letters came to the authors from people who wanted to know about the defects of particular products. Schlink and Chase, with financial assistance from the patrons of several liberal magazines and the editorial and technical assistance of friends, established and transformed a small White Plains, New York, consumer club into Consumers' Research, Incorporated, of New York City. Consumers' Research aspired to offer consumers the impartial services of "an economist, a scientist, an accountant, and goodness knows what more." Schlink expanded his confidential "Consumer's Club Commodity List" into a magazine, *Consumers' Research Bulletin*, that would "investigate, test and report reliably concerning hundreds of common commodities purchased." It would "accept no money or compensation of any kind from manufacturers, dealers, advertising agencies or other commercial enterprises." Subscriptions to his bulletin jumped from 565 in 1927 to 42,000 five years later. Recruiting many young writers and scientists into the enterprise, Schlink and Consumers' Research churned out not only the *Bulletin*, but dozens of consumer pamphlets, position papers, and books.[2]

In 1933, Schlink and Arthur Kallet, executive secretary on the board of Consumers' Research (and previously a co-worker with Schlink at the American Standards Association), released *100,000,000 Guinea Pigs: Dangers in Everyday Foods, Drugs and Cosmetics*. Kallet and Schlink used congressional interviews, public testimony, and files kept by Consumers' Research to flay such commonplace products as Bromo-Seltzer, Pepsodent, Kellogg's All-Bran, Crisco, Listerine, Sal-Hepatica, and Fleischmann's Yeast. They appealed for the mandatory disclosure of additives and ingredients for all foodstuffs, since, according to their view, weak laws left "a hundred million Americans . . . as unwitting test animals in a gigantic experiment with poisons, conducted by food, drug and cosmetic manufacturers."[3]

One of the best-selling books of the decade, *100,000,000 Guinea Pigs* spawned a wave of investigative "guinea pig" journalism unparalleled since the muckrakers. As Upton Sinclair's metaphor of people as illusioned immigrants suited life earlier in the century, the metaphor of people as guinea pigs seemed appropriate for the Depression. The metaphor conveyed a sense of exploitation by modern technological developments instead of benefit from them. Often repetitive and sometimes inaccurate or unfairly critical, the literature at its best surpassed the magnetism of muckraking literature through the immediacy and specificity of its prose. Along with other documentary protest of the 1930s—the short films of the Worker's Film and Photo League, or the photographs of Dorothea Lange, for example—the guinea pig books blended the passion of moral concern with sincere efforts to persuade the public of the necessity to use objective evidence to improve social conditions.[4]

The editors of the *Bulletin* tried to avoid sensationalism in the pages of the magazine itself. Printed in small type with little white space and few illustrations, the *Bulletin* looked like pages torn at random from a wholesale catalogue. Despite its serious purpose and lack of visual appeal, the spirit and approach of the magazine was lively, caustic, ironic, and informative.[5]

The amount of space devoted to rating products and to offering general guidance about buying was small at first. By 1934, however, it took up more than three-quarters of the magazine. Initially involved in writing for and helping to direct Consumers' Research, Stuart Chase soon left the organization for other interests. Consumers' Research thereafter conformed largely to the designs of Frederick Schlink. To fill magazine space, Schlink relied on material gleaned from former colleagues at the Bureau of Standards, from comments collected from readers, or from analytical tests performed by teachers at nearby universities. Schlink himself editorialized in favor of the establishment of a Department of Consumer Interests; better food and drug legislation; stricter legal tolerances for insecticide residues; better enforcement of existing drug laws; the need for stronger control of public utilities; and other topics. Frequently he reprinted items about consumer problems from other magazines.[6]

By 1935, Consumers' Research maintained a staff of more than 50, 200 outside consultants, and an impressive list of sponsors. Journalists Alexander Crosby of the *Nation*, Arthur Kellogg of *Survey*, and George Soule of the *New Republic* were among the sponsors, and wrote in their own magazines about the consumer movement and its relation to the recovery effort.[7]

As the staff grew larger and the readership grew more diverse, divisions over policies and future direction became common. There were arguments between the board members about how much of the resources of the organization should be spent for political or educational purposes, and about how much should be allocated for the improvement of the testing program.

Located first in White Plains and then in New York City, the organization moved in May 1933 to a remodeled two-story stone building and laboratory in Washington, New Jersey. According to Kallet, of the seventy employees who had been on staff in New York, only six moved to New Jersey. With Schlink's wife and close friends making up a majority of the board of directors, Schlink held close control of hiring, firing, and editorial and budgetary authority. His unyielding, paternal manner led to much bickering at the magazine. Between May 1933 and September 1935, the directors of Consumers' Research employed and then fired a succession of engineers, chemists, clerks, and stenographers.[8]

By the spring of 1935, dissatisfaction among the staff members had become serious enough to lead to several conferences covering job security and working conditions. In August, the workers formed the Consumers' Research Chapter of the Technical, Editorial and Office Assistants Union. The split between management and labor became public and formalized. When John Heasty, a chemist who had been appointed president of the union, asked for union recognition Schlink promptly fired him, along with two other union members. Early in September a strike broke out.

Arthur Kallet had been relatively inactive as a member of the Consumers' Research board of directors. Now he resigned his position and added his support to the cause of the strikers. Schlink, along with Mary Phillips, J. B. Matthews, and others on the board, used strikebreakers, legal injunctions, and armed detectives to maintain control of the offices and keep the magazine in operation. Caught in the middle of the dispute were the 55,000 subscribers to the *Bulletin*, who faced an unhappy dilemma—either to side with Schlink and his proven brand of capable consumer activism, or to support Kallet and the aggrieved workers at Consumers' Research.

This singular situation—revolutionary consumer activists at war with each other—contributed to the wry pleasure of such critics as *Business Week* and the *New York Times*. They took thinly concealed delight in the agonizing position of supposedly "anti-capitalist," "pro-labor" intellectuals

Consumers Research

STRIKE

Mass Meeting!
of subscribers and sympathizers
Town Hall, tomorrow night,
Thursday, Sept. 12th, 8:30 P.M.

SPEAKERS:
Heywood Broun
Frank Palmer Abraham Isserman
Arthur Kallet
(co author '100,000,000 Guinea Pigs')
— Admission Free —

2.1 The announcement of a meeting to discuss the Consumers' Research strike, placed in an unidentified New York newspaper, September 11, 1935. Courtesy of Consumers Union.

who now relied on the same weapons that J. B. Matthews recently had called "tools of big-corporation gangsterism." The strike cast doubt over the effectiveness of consumer-product testing and the ability of consumers to develop a common program of social reform and technological criticism.[9]

The last months of 1935 produced no solution to the strike, and little hope of compromise. Hoping to break the deadlock without further damage to themselves and their cause, the protesting workers and a group of subscribers petitioned for an impartial investigation by leaders of the liberal community to help settle the dispute. Reinhold Niebuhr, a religious philosopher deeply involved in the labor movement, presided over a committee which included Roger Baldwin of the American Civil Liberties Union, educator George Counts, and socialist Norman Thomas. The committee investigated the situation and concluded that, while the strikers deserved a measure of blame for prematurely cutting off their negotiations with management, the responsibility for the impasse rested with Consumers' Research. The organization would not succeed in reestablishing public confidence "or even the confidence of most of its subscribers, until it . . . adopted a policy of fair dealing with all its employees based upon collective bargaining in place of autocratic paternalism."[10]

A majority of the Consumers' Research board of directors had at first accused the strikers of being "dupes of business," and later, of having been infiltrated by communists. Schlink rejected arbitration by both the Niebuhr committee and the National Labor Relations Board. By December 1935, the strikers had abandoned the thought of returning to the New Jersey laboratories. Held together by Kallet, more than thirty workers determined to start a new publication, in the fused interests of consumers and workers, to be called *Consumers Union Reports*.

In the early months of 1936, the strikers and their sympathizers traded ideas about their proposed publication. By March, Consumers Union, Inc., had been chartered as a nonprofit corporation by the State of New York. While Consumers' Research rejected the idea of taking social conditions such as wages, hours, or factory surroundings into account when recommending products, the founders of Consumers Union decided that in order to aid people as consumers it would be necessary to help them "in their struggle as workers, to get an honest wage . . . by letting consumers know what products are manufactured under good labor conditions so that when possible they can favor them in making their purchases; by letting them know what products are produced under unfair conditions so that consumers can avoid such products." In contrast to the priority given to testing at Consumers' Research, at Consumers Union boycotts, educational activities, and political alliances with sup-

Consumers' Research
BULLETIN

Consumers' Research, Washington, N.J.

Vol. II. *(new series)*
(Vol. 5, No. 2 of the General Bulletin Series)   January, 1936   No. 4

Sources of Lead in Cocoa

Clinical Thermometers

Consumers Get a New "Protector"
by
Charles S. Wyand

The "Better Light-Better Sight" Campaign
The Power Trust Discovers Optometry

Ways and Means of Getting Fresh Coffee
*How Consumers Can Outwit the Coffee
Advertisers*

2.2   The front page of *Consumers' Research Bulletin*, published after strikers had left to form *Consumers Union Reports*. Note the combination of test reports and coverage of political developments. The *New "Protector"* referred to was a successor to the Consumer Advisory Board of the National Recovery Administration. Courtesy of Consumers' Research, Inc., Washington, N.J.

porters of consumer causes were to be undertaken as frequently as possible. Where Consumers' Research had created a sharp distinction between management and staff, Consumers Union determined to govern itself collectively.[11]

In May 1936, Consumers Union published the first issue of *Consumers Union Reports* magazine. Those liberal and radical readers who, for seven years, had come to admire the work of Consumers' Research and its founder Frederick Schlink now found two competing magazines—*Consumers' Research Bulletin* and *Consumers Union Reports*—claiming to represent the best interests of consumers. Within two years, *Consumer Reports*, as it became known, supplanted Schlink's publication as the most widely read and influential advocate of consumer-product testing.

Consumers Union

The successful formation of Consumers Union in 1936 resulted from the ability of the Consumers' Research strikers to attract support and attention from radical trade unionists, academicians, journalists, and segments of the liberal community. Led by Kallet, the strikers' committee leased offices off Union Square in New York City. It recruited an initial board of directors for Consumers Union that quickly became central to the decision making of the organization.* The board of directors in turn sought out a group of politically active intellectuals and potential benefactors as sponsors for their venture. Initial financial support came from hundreds

---

*Seven officers guided Consumers Union at the publication of the first issue of *Consumer Reports* in May 1936. Director Arthur Kallet received an engineering degree from the Massachusetts Institute of Technology in 1924 and joined Consumers' Research after meeting Frederick Schlink at the American Standards Association. Technical Supervisor Dewey Palmer, a former teacher of college physics, had worked at Consumers' Research while Kallet was executive secretary there. Secretary Frank Palmer, a founder of the Labor Press and previously an organizer for the Industrial Workers of the World, became interested in Consumers Union at the time of the strike at Consumers' Research. Vice-presidents James Gilman and Julius Hochman were both active with the labor and cooperative movements. Treasurer Adelaide Schulkind played a leading role in the work of the League for Mutual Aid and other labor-oriented philanthropies. President Colston Warne, a professor at Amherst College, studied economics with Veblen's friend and supporter Herbert Davenport at Cornell, and wrote his doctoral thesis about the cooperative movement for Paul Douglas at the University of Chicago. Warne had been active in labor education, civil liberties work, and in the "people's lobby" of socialist Benjamin Marsh.

of small contributions to the strike fund, from advance subscriptions to the proposed publication, and from one large grant of $1500 from an earlier patron of Consumers' Research.[12]

The directors at first wanted to operate the organization as a cooperative, socialist experiment. Decision making was to be guided as far as possible by the will of the member-subscribers, as determined from questionnaires and through membership meetings. Ballot-questionnaires were mailed every year. They offered subscribers the chance to vote for members of the board and to indicate the topics that they hoped the organization would explore. For the first year of operation, everyone from the secretaries to the editors received the same weekly salary. In March 1937, however, Kallet and the board reached the conclusion that in spite of their radical ideals, it would be necessary to pay varying salaries that were "competitive with capitalist organizations," "in order that the organization might engage and retain the best possible technicians, editorial, promotion and secretarial staff."[13]

For the early numbers of the magazine, Dr. Harold Aaron, a friend of Kallet's who had been involved in the advocacy of socialized medicine, prepared copy that discussed common medical problems such as indigestion and constipation. Alexander Crosby and Frank Palmer, reporters attracted to the idea of a consumer-labor alliance, began piecing together information about conditions of labor in various industries. Free-lance writers contributed articles concerning utility bills, transportation costs, cooperative buying plans, legislative proposals, and other topics.[14]

Dewey Palmer, a former teacher of physics who was appointed technical supervisor of the new organization, communicated with testing laboratories, private chemists, the Bureau of Standards, and the Department of Agriculture to acquire information about techniques of testing and to arrange for outside testing work to be done. Because of the perpetually weak financial condition of Consumers Union during the 1930s, the technical work generally was confined to the exploration of items that would be inexpensive to test, either by the everyday use of the staff, or else through experiments in the laboratory. Meeting those criteria were items such as soap, suntan lotion, silk and rayon stockings, canned foods,

---

Other members of the first board of directors were Robert Brady, economist; Heywood Broun, journalist and leader of the Newspaper Guild; Osmond K. Fraenkel, attorney; John Heasty, a staff representative on the board; Charles Marlies, professor of chemistry at the City College of New York; A. Phillip Randolph, leader of the Brotherhood of Sleeping Car Porters; Bernard Reis, accountant; and Rose Schneiderman, president of the Women's Trade Union League.

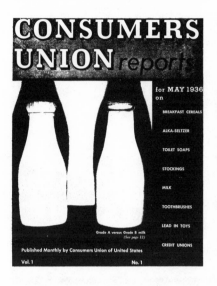

2.3   Prewar covers of *Consumer Reports,* including the first issue, May 1936. (A) A cover that reported charges against *Good Housekeeping* (from a reprint of the September 1939 issue); (B) the March 1939 issue emphasized the thoroughness and energy with which CU rated a product as common as soap; (C) an issue that contained Consumers Union's reaction to the attacks of J. B. Matthews before the House Un-American Activities Committee. Courtesy of Consumers Union.

2.4 An early legal battle that helped CU establish its right to protect its reports from unauthorized commercial uses was the Doeskin Products case. Although *Consumer Reports* had not rated Doeskin Sanitary Napkins as superior to other brands, the company said as much on its packages and in its advertising. Consumers Union brought its case before a federal court and won. Courtesy of Consumers Union.

pencils, shirts, tissue paper, shoes, and razor blades. Which cereal provided the most bulk for the money? How could a person penetrate advertising claims to find durable clothing or wholesome food? Was Grade B milk just as safe to drink as the more expensive Grade A variety? Those and other questions were approached on the basis of common sense and product testing.[15]

There were serious difficulties with the quality of the early technical work. Dr. Charles Marlies, the only scientist on the board of directors in 1938, reflected the feeling of the technical supervisor and other personnel that technical work had not been permitted to grow with the organization. Of fifty members of the staff of Consumers Union in February 1939, only seven were technical employees. Perhaps the low point in the morale of the testing staff occurred after May 1938, when *Consumer Reports* mistakenly accused the Libby Company of allowing its canned peas to contain poisonous belladonna, "deadly nightshade." In fact, the debris inside the cans was harmless. At the same time, much of the energy of staff members went toward taking part in political affairs and reporting about them. These activities included testimony before various municipal, state, and federal trade-law hearings, the preparation of a consumer's exhibit at the New York World's Fair, labor movement picketing, support for anti-Fascist boycotts, and promotional drives among the poor. Meanwhile, product testing was being handled in an unsystematic and sometimes unscientific way. Discouraged by the trend away from scientific work, Dewey Palmer resigned from his post as technical supervisor in 1939. Concerned that the testing process was being subordinated to political advocacy, Professor Charles Marlies left the board of directors in the same year.[16]

The political action that Consumers Union staff members took part in during the late 1930s helped to attract many liberal readers and patrons, but it became clear to the board that the development of an effective testing program should not be neglected in favor of a preoccupation with consumer activism. Acknowledging the crucial importance to Consumers Union of reputable scientific ratings, the board took steps to improve the situation. Kallet assumed greater responsibility for the development of the testing program. He reported to members of Consumers Union in 1939 that a new laboratory was being established to provide facilities for chemical, electrical, bacteriological, and textile testing. A short-lived West Coast office was set up to test the particular brands and to serve the special needs of western subscribers. To build support for Consumers Union within the scientific community, Kallet and Warne in December 1939 arranged a joint conference between the Cambridge-Boston branch of the American Association of Scientific Workers (AASW) and the members of Consumers Union. At that conference, "CU admitted that its testing facilities were inadequate, that at times reports were based on unsupported opinion, and that mistakes had been made in spite of honest intent." Nevertheless the AASW offered to help improve the situation by furnishing technical advice to consumer organizations and to make arrangements for the testing of certain products. Consumers Union worked hard to improve its testing routine.[17]

By June 1939, membership in Consumers Union had risen to a new high of 85,000. As the organization grew and become geographically more diverse, the sponsors and board were surprised to discover that, despite membership drives targeted at trade-union groups, despite special low-cost subscriptions, and despite test projects that had been planned to meet the needs of poor families, *Consumer Reports* reached middle- and upper-income consumers more frequently than those with low incomes. About 5 percent of the membership in 1939 earned less than $1000 per year, while about 13 percent earned above $5000. Indeed, the largest groups of readers in that year were professional workers—especially teachers, school administrators, and engineers. The consumer movement as a whole did not fare differently. A Gallup survey in 1940 indicated that only 12 percent of lower-income families had even heard of a consumer movement, contrasted with 48 percent of upper-income groups. Both the utilitarian philosophy and the practical buying advice that the movement offered appeared to be of interest predominantly to the middle class.[18]

The magazine grew in spite of the strident opposition of the business community and the commercial press. Claiming that consumer product testing represented an unfair and subversive attack upon legitimate advertising, more than sixty newspapers and magazines, including Hearst, Crowell, Scribner's, and *New York Times* publications, refused to sell their advertising space to Consumers Union. The *Women's Home Companion* in 1938 called Consumers Union "a burrowing shrimp undermining the American Way of Life." Angered by attacks made by Consumers Union on the value of the Good Housekeeping Seal of Approval, a spokeswoman for *Good Housekeeping* accused *Consumer Reports* of prolonging the Depression by destroying confidence in the institution of advertising.[19]

J. B. Matthews, an apostate Marxist and a codirector who had been with Frederick Schlink at Consumers' Research, testified in 1938 to the subversiveness of Consumers Union before a House committee investigating subversive activities, chaired by Martin Dies (D-Texas). Consumers Union, Matthews charged, had developed because communists had been unsuccessful at subverting Consumers' Research. Certainly Kallet,

Warne, Bernard Reis, and other members of the staff and board never tried to make their radical consumer philosophy a secret. They and many of the workers at Consumers Union at that time held diverse forms of radical political views. But the guiding hands at Consumers Union were careful to steer the organization and the magazine on a nonpartisan course. The variety of political views at the organization, the absence of any political creed within the pages of *Consumer Reports,* and the defamatory way in which Matthews and others levied their accusations all led the public and several members of the Dies Committee itself to discount the allegations.[20]

The emergency preparations for the Second World War which began late in 1939 changed the direction of the consumer movement and slowed the expansion of Consumers Union. CU initiated efforts to keep track of problems of civilian supply and, after Pearl Harbor, began to publish *Bread and Butter,* a popular weekly newsletter (circulation approximately fifty-four thousand) that traced problems including price controls, housing shortages, quality deterioration, and other domestic economic developments. CU launched efforts to bring wartime consumer education into elementary- and secondary-school classrooms. Led by Colston Warne, the organization urged the government to prevent corporations from taking tax deductions for products that they advertised with funds appropriated from government war contracts.[21]

Subscriptions to *Consumer Reports* during the war leveled off. The magazine became more difficult to produce. Employees were drafted or took positions in war industries. By 1944, with the induction of the chief technician into the army, the laboratory staff consisted of two chemists and an assistant. The overwhelming majority of testing work was given to outside consultants.[22]

Beginning late in 1945, deferred demand for consumer goods expanded with the demobilization of the armed forces and the reconversion of defense industries. New automobiles, durable appliances, and innovations that had developed from wartime technological advances began to appear on the civilian market. In search of honest evaluations of those products, an increasing number of consumers turned to *Consumer Reports.* In 1946, more than fifty-six hundred readers asked the magazine to rate all kinds of goods and services, but especially electric refrigerators, vacuum cleaners, automobiles, and radios. Subscriptions increased from under ninety thousand in 1945 to above four hundred thousand in 1950, with a corresponding increase in revenue that allowed Consumers Union to expand its staff and testing program.[23]

With evaluations of some 1,793 brands and models of 116 types of products during 1949, Consumers Union reached a new peak in the rate, quality, and systematization of its process of rating. Consumers Union had hired a new technical director, chemist Morris Kaplan, who helped to split the technical work into divisions including electronics, textiles, appliances, chemistry, foods, and special projects. Kallet authorized a large expansion of the automobile-testing program. The home economics department of Cornell University agreed to help to test sewing machines for *Consumer Reports,* and the Department of Agriculture permitted an employee of Consumers Union to work under its supervision in Washington on the grading of canned food.[24]

Accustomed to directing its ratings to low-income consumers who sought basic necessities, the magazine found itself serving an audience of consumers with time and money to spend selecting luxuries. Much of that readership and some of the new personnel disregarded the political context in which the magazine had been founded and looked only for answers to narrow questions about the products being manufactured. Along with the encouragement that the new prosperity gave to *Consumer Reports* to serve as a buying guide, an anticommunist, antisocialist atmosphere was developing which led the magazine to modify its coverage of legislative activity, its reports about labor, and its criticism of advertising.

The officers and most of the staff remained dedicated to a broad conception of consumer interests, but Kallet particularly worried that the work of the previous decade and the allegations of J. B. Matthews had left Consumers Union vulnerable to charges of being subversive of free enterprise. Concerned by attacks from local Better Business Bureaus and by the suppression by some school boards of *Consumer Reports* for classroom use, Kallet prepared to steer Consumers Union away from charges of radicalism. He arranged a more conservative membership for the board of directors. Deflecting the accusation that "members" of CU might be communists or radicals, he secured a revision in the bylaws to distinguish between "members" and "subscribers." The wartime weekly *Bread and Butter* in 1947 was incorporated with *Consumer Reports* to become an occasional feature with the more neutral title, "Economics for Consumers." Relaxing its ties with labor, the magazine let lapse its coverage—"postponed" since 1938—of labor conditions in the industries whose products it rated. In those ways the staff tried to satisfy new readers, defuse the issue of radicalism, and yet preserve its consumer-oriented ideology.[25]

Consumers Union reformulated the themes of the consumerism of the 1930s to meet the concerns of postwar, middle-class America. While the magazine showed less than its traditional interest in such labor legislation as the Taft-Hartley Act, strong editorial statements criticized the failure of the Truman administration to cope with inflation through effective price controls. Formerly *Consumer Reports* had placed a premium in its ratings upon simplicity and economy, but after the war, factors of convenience and safety received greater consideration in the ratings. During the 1930s the magazine had tested items such as milk, soap, or bread and found that many low-cost products were identical to higher-priced goods. After 1945, as the tests themselves became more refined, the reports emphasized distinctions of purity or freshness that earlier tests had ignored.[26]

A thriving publishing organization, Consumers Union during the 1950s faced problems common to that trade, and other difficulties unique to a scientific group that published the results of its own research. Attorneys successfully protected the ratings of the magazine from unauthorized use by commercial interests and established the ability of the organization to report the results of its tests truthfully—including the mention of brand names—without a paralyzing fear of legal recrimination. In spite of numerous lawsuits filed by unhappy manufacturers, Consumers Union during its first three decades did not lose any case or reach a single unfavorable settlement outside of court. In 1950 Consumers Union retained an advertising agency to help it with newsstand promotion, a development greeted with bemused derision by other agencies and magazines. The directors tried to solve institutional problems such as pension plans, paid vacation time, and retirement benefits for management employees. Encountering difficult labor relations in 1951, segments of the management suspected District 65 CIO|(now independent) of communist infiltration. After an emotionally disruptive strike and lockout, matters were settled through a new contract with the Newspaper Guild. By 1954, Consumers Union had succeeded in improving its labor relations, in clearing its name from the House Un-American Activities Committee's list of subversive organizations, and in establishing permanent headquarters in a refurbished, rambling, former optical equipment factory in the industrial section of Mount Vernon, New York.[27]

Internal relations at Consumers Union during the 1950s were not harmonious. Differences arose between technical engineers and editorial writers, between activists of different stripes and those committed to product testing more narrowly defined, and among the personnel who were involved at each stage of preparation of the reports for publication. Those disputes frequently were reflected at the level of the board of directors, where budgetary authority rested. Colston Warne, an active critic of advertising and advocate of consumer representation in government, became a spokesman for more ambitious product testing and for more wide-ranging consumer activity at CU. Kallet, concerned with the coordination and oversight of daily operations in Mount Vernon, asked for increased appropriations for the testing program itself. In April 1957, after frequent skirmishes with Warne and with Treasurer Bernard Reis, Kallet lost his position as executive director.[28]

As Consumers Union proved to be capable of weathering external pressures and internal storms, its magazine became a fixture in the con-

2.5   (A) Colston Warne addressing an economics class during the 1940s; (B) Dexter Masters speaking to a joint conference of CU and the American Association of Scientific Workers, July 1940; (C) Irving Michelson, chemist, shortly after he began work at CU in 1947. Courtesy of Consumers Union.

sumer movement and a topic for discussion among sociologists and students of the affluent American life-style. "The large circulation of *Consumer Reports* and *Consumers' Bulletin* is significant," wrote William Whyte in 1955. "There may be only a few subscribers in any one neighborhood, but they have an impact over and above their numbers. The housewife who has just digested a report on, say, ironers, has a conversational gambit that is sure to be exercised when she chats in the alleyways with her friends." "What Dr. Spock is to freshman parents, the Consumers Union is to bewildered housewives," noted a business reporter for the *New York Times* in 1959. Americans—particularly women, it was suggested—would derive as much self-assurance, as much timely wisdom, as much comforting advice from *Consumer Reports* as their faith in CU's scientific method could sustain.[29]

Studies suggested to businessmen that a good rating in *Consumer Reports* could improve their volume of sales dramatically, and that a poor rating could spell disaster. When Consumers Union in 1956 reported that several electric fans had inadequately guarded blades, for example, poor sales of those brands led manufacturers to improve their products. Spokesmen for Maytag washers and Volkswagen cars attributed their penetration of oligopolistic markets to superior ratings by the magazine.[30]

Others questioned the desirability and applicability of any ratings technique that omitted or discounted nonutilitarian motives for buying, such as style, fashion, or status. "This pretzeled economics dished out by *Consumer Reports* states that there's something immoral [about making] . . . consumers consume any goods sold except for strictly replacement or utility needs," wrote one businessman. "If the human race attempted to live by the credo of this primitive theme, it would still be in the throes of trying to invent the wheel by the flickering light of a cave fire." Satires of *Consumer Reports* ridiculed the magazine by claiming to subject ordinary products to obviously inappropriate tests, for example trying to float cars or to use toasters as sewing machines. Other parodies pretended to test products that consumers would be unlikely to care about. *Humbug* magazine published "*Consumer Retorts*," with "best buys in confetti, seismographs and rickshaws." Some spoofs took CU's method to an outrageous extreme by rating unique, personal, intimate experiences. *Jackpot* magazine, a pornographic venture, claimed in 1957 to have checked "more than 550 girls in the high, low and medium-priced fields." A British comedy group rated the major faiths against one another in a skit titled "*Consumer Reports* Looks at Religion." During the late 1950s and 1960s, light humor and serious criticism implied that the urge to quantify and to objectify might invade every aspect of human behavior.[31]

While some challenged the desirability of the ratings technique,

2.6 In 1954, Consumers Union established its main editorial and testing facility in this former optical plant in Mount Vernon, N.Y. Courtesy of Consumers Union.

2.7 A solemn staff meeting at Consumers Union during the mid-1950s. *Clockwise:* Morris Kaplan, technical director; Jean Whitehill, editorial; Dorothy Walsh, librarian; Arthur Kallet, executive director; Lawrence (Pete) Crooks, autos; Florence Mason, librarian; Madeline Ross, assistant to the executive director. Courtesy of Consumers Union.

This article is dedicated to the proposition that all things are *not* created equal—not by today's manufacturers, anyway. But the American Consumer has an ally in his never-ending battle with poor craftsmanship, shoddy merchandise and Giant Economy Size Packages that are never more than half full...mainly, the Impartial Test Panels. Those dedicated experts who break down a product before they break down and tell us all about it in magazines like....

CONDEMNER REPORTS

OCTOBER 1969 / MANUFACTURERS HATE US SO WE GET / NO ADVERTISING / 50 CENTS

Razors and Blades
Use-Tested by a special 500-Man CR Panel

Styptic Pencils
Use-Tested by the same 500-Man CR Panel right after the Razors and Blades tests

Electric Hot Plates
Almost all models had poor insulation and none had adequate, heat-resistant handles

Burn Ointments
An unscheduled report necessitated by the tests of those %&$#@¢!! Electric Hot Plates

Mixers and Blenders
Our special 26-Man Team tests most brands

The New Long Ties
A special CR Report shows why men who use mixers and blenders should not wear them

Fire Extinguishers
None of the Fire Extinguisher Units that we tested could adequately control a fire

New Construction
CR examines new building construction as it searches for a new home after making those %&$#@¢#!! Fire Extinguisher tests

ARTIST: BOB CLARKE   WRITER: DICK DE BARTOLO   PHOTOGRAPHY: BY IRVING SCHILD

2.8 One of many parodies of *Consumer Reports*, this in *Mad* magazine, January 1970. Reproduced courtesy of *Mad*, © 1969 by E. C. Publications, Inc.

others doubted that the irrational behavior of consumers was in fact affected by *Consumer Reports*. A professor of psychology at Michigan State University suggested that consumers received emotional satisfaction from reading the reports and *thinking* themselves logical, rather than from actually following the logic that *CR* offered. Did consumers understand what they read in *Consumer Reports* and act according to their improved awareness? Or did the guidance of a "scientific authority" bring to the public a new kind of faith, one similar in many respects to the confidence that advertisers tried to instill? As a buying ritual for an age of science, a consultation with the scientific ratings in *Consumer Reports* might sanctify consumption, rather than make it more functional or efficient.[32]

Those who were more intimately connected with the magazine expressed additional concerns about its influence. Columnist Sidney Margolius and statistician William Pabst, both members of the board during the 1950s, found that Consumers Union used inconsistent criteria to decide what products to test, what rating schemes to use, or how many samples of each product to purchase. In a searching, confidential report written for the board of directors in 1956, economist Robert Brady asked whether there was any plan or comprehensiveness to the economic, medical, or technical coverage in *Consumer Reports*. Brady wondered if the continual selection of best-selling, national brands in preference to minor or regional ones had the effect of promoting industrial concentration; or whether the regulatory and interventionist approaches that the magazine sometimes recommended to control monopolies or high prices were in the best long-run interest of the consuming public. Perhaps CU's accustomed methods of deciding what to rate and how to test needed to be changed. "We have become a major national organization," observed Dexter Masters, the editor who succeeded Kallet as executive director, "but we are proceeding . . . according to patterns [of policy] set years ago from which we are attempting to draw more than we can."[33]

By Consumers Union's twenty-fifth anniversary in 1961, those who had been associated with the magazine since its earliest days looked with some puzzlement at the phenomenal success of their organization, and at the still-chaotic state of the American marketplace. The circulation of the magazine exceeded eight hundred thousand. Publication income approached four million dollars. "Unquestionably, CU's Board and its staff have not been as experimental as they should have been . . . we little comprehended the expansion and subsequent community acceptance which would ensue . . .," Colston Warne admitted. "A thing that haunts me, and I am sure it worries the staff of CU," wrote Robert Lynd, "is that the policeman's effort to catch up with crime tends to trap him in the endless pursuit of only a token portion of the abuses he seeks to prevent

. . . none of us should have illusions that the policing of misdeeds, after the event, is affecting the hare and hound race of merchandising."[34]

By the early 1980s, the number of subscribers to *Consumer Reports* exceeded two and a quarter million. Regardless of the greater number of activities that this increased readership allowed, those who guided Consumers Union understood that they could hardly provide a truly adequate counterweight to the pressures of commercial advertising or to the influence placed on the government by business interests. Nevertheless, in product testing they had found a method of technological and social criticism that reflected trust in the objectivity of science and confidence in the ability of the public to be moved by scientific evidence dispassionately presented. Through product testing, they believed, consumer reform might transform the progressive social movements of the past. Product testing might help to make reform a rational, empirical, objective, impartial, unsentimental, effective, scientific process.

CHAPTER III

The Risk of Smoking: Verifying the Tradition of Temperance

DURING THE EARLY MONTHS OF 1936, the guiding hands at Consumers Union met often in the office of Arthur Kallet to consider the problems of their magazine. Looking for new subjects to investigate, they decided at one meeting to consider a report about cigarettes. That hesitant beginning developed into a persistent concern. During the following thirty years Consumers Union published more than thirty reports, one hundred pages of text and ratings, dozens of reprints, and a major book about smoking.[1]

For the first fifteen years of publication, *Consumer Reports* denigrated or ignored previous discussions about tobacco. The staff was alienated by prosmoking propaganda sponsored by the tobacco industry and suspicious of antismoking literature in the coffin-nail tradition. The editors dealt with tobacco as an ordinary commodity and divorced their writing from the moralism, sensationalism, and bias that they believed had discredited earlier discussions. After the product testers came to accept the dangers of smoking on scientific grounds, they then faced a difficult problem shared by many reformers: the need to translate the conviction of their organization into reaction and commitment by the public. The history of antismoking movements and of the magazine's involvement in the smoking controversy reflects the evolution of American reform strategies and the growing receptivity of Americans to appeals based on scientific evidence.

The Antismoking Tradition

Nineteenth-century Americans did not consider smoking as dangerous as drinking. Smoking did not appear to lower inhibitions, interfere with working ability, serve as a social equalizer, or produce a state that resembled drunkenness. Tobacco shops usually looked more like quiet stores than saloons or bars. Some forms of tobacco (like certain kinds of alcohol) earned less social approval than others; but snuff, chewing plugs, cigars, and pipes did not differ enough in potency to suggest permitting some while prohibiting others. Unlike alcohol, furthermore, the various ways of using tobacco corresponded weakly to distinctions of class or status. Before President John Quincy Adams gave up the habit, for example, he believed he had been "addicted" to both smoking and chewing.[2]

Antebellum tobacco temperance drew much of its leadership from repentant smokers and religious leaders who fostered their own sense of moral authority and control as they encouraged voluntary and perfectionist self-improvement. Moses Stuart of Andover Seminary did not "place the use of tobacco in the same scale with ardent spirits," but he thought it operated "on the temper and moral character of men" by creating a thirst for liquor, alluring men to grogshops, and contributing to delinquency. George Trask formed the American Anti-Tobacco Society in 1848, to solicit pledges of "immediate and entire reformation" of an "injurious . . . slovenly, sluttish and disgusting habit." Many towns passed fire laws against smoking in wooden buildings or public places during these years, but the concern of temperance workers was primarily individualist and moralist in scope and approach.[3]

Searching for ways to emphasize the importance of prohibition, crusaders tried to show that habitual use marked one step on a road to greater ruin. Like twentieth-century arguments that linked marijuana to heroin, antitobacco propaganda alleged that tobacco led to alcohol through a culture of immorality. Reverend A. McAllister explained that, although every lover of tobacco was not a slave to rum, *"yet almost every drunkard is a slave to tobacco."* "Show me a genuine blackguard . . . who is not a lover of tobacco in some shape," wrote Horace Greeley, "and I will agree to find you two white blackbirds."[4]

Testimony by doctors reinforced moral arguments. In 1857 a British doctor wrote in the journal *Lancet* that tobacco acted on the mind by producing drowsiness and irritability, and on the respiratory organs "by causing consumption, haemoptysis, and inflammatory condition of the mucous membrane of the larynx, trachea, and bronchae, ulceration of the larynx, short irritable cough [and] hurried breathing." The *Lancet*'s description of the dangerous effects of tobacco was perhaps excessively technical for the general public. Dr. R. D. Mussey of the Miami Medical

FOR THE MILLIONS.

LITTLE DICK'S FIRST ATTEMPT TO BE A MAN!

Says the venerable Dr. Woods, " Once when I was young, and knew nothing of the danger, I was tempted by an old chewer to use it, which I did for a little while; in consequence, I was suddenly sick and intoxicated, and was taken up as dead. The poison was as nearly fatal as it could be consistently with remaining life."

"Tobacco is an Indian Weed,
And 't was the Devil that sowed the seed."

Little Charlie poisoned by his father's quid, which he had swallowed; the doctor pumps it from his stomach, and exclaims, "Accursed tobacco!"

In Roxbury, an Irish woman, having heard that tobacco steeped in milk would operate as a vermifuge, administered it to her own child, causing its death in less than an hour and a half.

REMEDY.

Reader, 1. Never use it yourself. 2. Banish it from your families and premises. 3. Purify the church. 4. Rebuke the manufacture and sale of it. 5. Look after schools, and save the young. 6. Sign and circulate this Pledge : I HEREBY PLEDGE MYSELF TO ABSTAIN FROM THE USE OF TOBACCO, IN ALL FORMS, TOTALLY AND FOREVER.

Anti-Tobacco Tract Depository, Fitchburg, Mass. — GEO. TRASK.

3.1 A page from the *Anti-Tobacco Journal* of George Trask, 1860. Trask's chief objective was soliciting pledges to refrain from using tobacco, rather than obtaining a law to prohibit its sale. Courtesy of Arents Collection, The New York Public Library, Astor, Lenox and Tilden Foundations.

College, however, performed a more graphic "proof" of its harm when he rubbed "oil of tobacco" (probably nicotine) on the tongue of a large cat. "The animal uttered piteous cries and began to froth at the mouth," he reported. "In one minute the pupils of the eyes were dilated and the animal fell upon the side senseless and breathless, and the heart had ceased to beat."[5]

Exploiting the growing captivation of the public with hydropathy, health cures, and "scientific" revelations, essayists circulated and imitated Mussey's experiments with nicotine. In reaction to various wrenching accounts of dying animals, wilting plants, and suffocating insects, readers fixed upon the image of doctors and ministers methodically killing life to convert smokers. The mask of clinical observation allowed writers to shock the refined sensibilities of middle-class readers in otherwise unacceptable ways.

Pamphlets and tracts of the antebellum period yielded to treatises, testimonials, and first-hand accounts of tobacco's toll. Emphasizing the menace of tobacco to the proper upbringing of children, writers showed more care for entertaining their readers than for persuading them. Anti-smoking testimony often consisted of disorganized commentaries by school principals, ministers, or members of the social elite. Authors sandwiched reasonable discussions of the possibility of transmitting disease by spitting, of the problems of tobacco "cough," "tobacco heart," or even cancer, between stories such as that of a doctor who knew of two families "where in each case there is a nest of little children rendered idiots by the tobacco habits of their parents," or tales of babies poisoned by sleeping in the beds of fathers who smoked. Unusual cases or isolated incidents sufficed to link tobacco with the impairment of health, poor academic performance, familial irresponsibility, and miscellaneous antisocial behavior.[6]

The consumption of tobacco trailed the growth of the population for the first part of the nineteenth century, but after the Civil War per capita use began to increase. By 1880 Americans annually consumed about five and one-half pounds for every person above the age of fourteen. With the perfection of cigarette rolling machines in 1883, the cigarette became cheaper and easier to mass-produce than cigars or chewing plugs. Cigarettes also smelled better, were more hygienic, and were more rapidly consumed. They gained ground steadily in urban, industrial America.[7]

Like other variations on older ways of life that were made possible by new technology, cigarette smoking made more rapid headway among the young than the old, and widened the cultural and generational tensions that existed at the end of the century. Accustomed to cigars, pipes, and chewing tobacco, the older part of the population found it easy to generalize about the consumers of white paper. Critics declared the cigarette "fiend" to be young, irresponsible, licentious, disrespectful, and rebellious. That characterization became self-fulfilling when parents, schools, and churches translated their predispositions into rules. Cigarettes symbolized elements that corrupted youth and were in the process of subverting American values.[8]

Alarmed by initial increases in the sales of cigarettes, by further gains made as a result of the introduction of mild-blend tobaccos by Camel (1913), and also by health campaigns against cuspidors, the producers of cigars organized efforts to discredit what they called "coffin nails." Cigarette makers were said to lace tobacco with opium and morphine, to bleach rolling paper with arsenic and white lead, and to mix burnt cigar stumps into their blends. Fearful of having the values of the white community corrupted by a habit that allegedly spread from the black neighborhoods, a Philadelphia paper contended that leading doctors condemned cigarette smoking as "one of the most destructive evils that ever befell the youth of any country." A New York city magistrate declared that ninety-nine out of one hundred of the boys who came before him charged with crime had their fingers "disfigured by yellow cigarette stain." Temperance workers, ministers, and industrialists joined cigar makers to indict the habit. Some religious leaders advocated the prohibition of all tobacco, but cigarettes became the common ground of prohibitionist concern.[9]

For progressives the economic case against cigarettes became critical to the antismoking argument. Unlike the competitive craft structure of cigar manufacturing, the cigarette business consisted of a few firms that by 1899 had been consolidated by James Duke into the American Tobacco Company, popularly assailed as the Tobacco Trust. Bothered by the concentration of the industry, Theodore Roosevelt in 1906 took action against the trust under the Sherman Act. Five years later the Supreme Court dissolved the American Tobacco Company into four parts. The retail price of cigarettes did not decline subsequently, but the case brought to attention the size of the industry and the aggregate cost of national addiction. Professor Henry W. Farnam of Yale computed the sum people wasted on smoking in the years prior to 1914 and announced that it drained citizens of money that otherwise might have gone toward social improvement. According to Farnam, the manufactured value of tobacco exceeded the value of bread, women's clothing, copper, automobiles, and petroleum. William B. Bailey, a Yale statistician, emphasized that the amount spent on tobacco constituted twice the sum devoted to the common school system. What earlier reformers perceived as a problem of individual weakness susceptible to the power of moral suasion now appeared to be a social problem that demanded a political remedy as well.[10]

Patterned after antisaloon leagues, anticigarette leagues began to emerge after 1890. Lucy Gaston Page, Carrie Nation, and others received support from the National Education Association and the National Congress of Parents and Teachers, and between 1897 and 1921 the leagues managed to secure hundreds of local ordinances which restricted the sale or importation of cigarettes. Twelve southern and western states prohibited their sale entirely, and every state but two passed laws against the smoking of cigarettes by minors. The Tennessee State Supreme Court ruled that cigarettes properly could be regulated through the police powers of government, since their use was "always harmful, never beneficial." The United States Supreme Court supported that reasoning, and wrote that it would be "shutting its eyes to reality" if it ignored the fact that a "belief in their deleterious effects, particularly upon young people," had become general.[11]

Anticigarette sentiment reached new peaks in the years prior to the entrance of the United States into the First World War, at the same time that the consumption of cigarettes soared. Cigar smoker Thomas Edison theorized that the principal injurious agent in cigarettes was the paper wrapper, whose combustion led to "permanent degeneration of brain cells." Henry Ford filled his pamphlet series *The Case Against the Little*

—Thomas in "Detroit News"

3.2   According to Henry Ford and Thomas Edison, smoking destroyed initiative—the smoker was "Not a Live Wire." From Ford, *The Case Against the Little White Slaver* (1914), courtesy of Arents Collection, The New York Public Library, Astor, Lenox and Tilden Foundations.

White Slaver with similar testimonials. An editor of *Success* magazine wrote that smoking cigarettes was "no longer a moral question; the great business world has taken it up as a deadly enemy of advancement and achievement." E. H. Harriman, president of the Union Pacific Railroad, declared that he would "just as soon think of getting employees out of the insane asylum as to employ cigarette users."[12]

If failure, adolescence, commonness, or effeminancy were linked to smoking during the Progressive era, those images faded in the years during and after the First World War. Exploiting the taste for cigarettes that soldiers had acquired in Europe, sophisticated advertising campaigns promoted the idea that it was virile and modern to smoke new blends of tobacco. Women began to smoke, and in contrast to social feminists of earlier days who had worked to discourage smoking, feminists in the 1920s considered smoking part of their new image—a symbol of equality, power, and sexual freedom.[13]

Hoping to counteract the influence of advertising and worried by the growing social acceptance of the habit, a "Committee to Study the Tobacco Problem" in 1918 began to sponsor the dissemination of "data regarding tobacco and its effects, particularly physiological and economic." The doctors, economists, statisticians, and college athletic directors on the committee tried without success to put the antismoking argument on a sound scientific footing.[14]

Despite eminent committees and a few interesting monographs, antismokers scarcely dented the steadily rising popularity of cigarettes. The first generation of cigarette smokers had reached political maturity by the mid-1920s: "smoke-filled rooms" contained more cigarette than cigar smoke for the first time. Prohibition laws, which always suffered from nonenforcement and bootlegging, disappeared as state governments realized that they could profit by taxing cigarettes. Cigarette manufacturers developed political and economic leverage because of the popularity of their product and the money they spent on local and national advertising. Laws in many states continued to forbid minors from buying cigarettes, but those referring to adults all had been repealed by 1928.[15]

Exceeding an average of fifteen hundred cigarettes per person per year by 1929, the sale of cigarettes outdistanced cigars, pipes, and chewing tobacco combined. Advertising expenditures for the industry exceeded $75 million in 1931. On billboards, in the print media, and over the radio, Camels, Luckies, Chesterfields, Old Golds, and later Philip Morris fought to capture new smokers and create defections from their rivals. The techniques used to promote the national brands set new levels of sophistication for public relations. Using advice gathered from consultants versed in Freudian psychology, George W. Hill spent $19 million in

3.3   Cartoon suggesting that cigarette advertising would lead
a proper gentleman upward on "The Narcotic Stairs." Un-
catalogued broadside, courtesy of Arents Collection, The New
York Public Library, Astor, Lenox and Tilden Foundations.

one year to convince women to "reach for a Lucky instead of a sweet."
Caught in the blast of promotional static, the voice of a few antismokers
and medical researchers faded away.[16]

By 1936, the year the first issue of *Consumer Reports* appeared, the
opponents of tobacco despaired of retarding the accelerating sales of cigarettes. The antismoking argument languished from its association with the
failure of prohibition and its link to progressive and Victorian moral
values. If the discouragement of smoking did not wither completely, it
could only be attributed to the lingering doubts of the public and to the
residual strength of progressive thought. Despite the image that the tobacco sellers tried to project, there were still some who believed that
smoking could be a debilitating as well as a satisfying habituation.

The Cigarette as a Commodity:
A Critique by Consumers

The writers at *Consumers Reports* initially became interested in testing cigarettes for reasons unrelated to the arguments of antismokers. The chief object of the consumer advocates was, quite simply, to judge each brand against the others. Most of the staff and members of the board smoked regularly. The magazine first described smoking as one of the "most widely used and misrepresented" practices in modern culture, but not as one of the most dangerous. For an organization surviving on a shoestring, such reporting on cigarettes offered a relatively simple and inexpensive way to probe problems of the marketplace and to extend the utility of consumer research.[17]

Subscribing to the philosophical relativism that prevailed on the left during the Depression, the staff and board held to the general view that beneficial social planning required the accommodation to, not the control or suppression of, "natural" or genuine human needs. This naturalism provided the consumer activists with a point of departure for making ethical and moral decisions. Since the use of tobacco had saturated the nation so rapidly and thoroughly, it reflected, in the view of economist Jessie Coles, a "primary buying motive," a demand determined by true psychological necessity. Robert Lynd argued that a fertile field for sociological analysis existed wherever the current culture cramped or distorted "the quest of considerable numbers of persons for satisfaction." That belief accorded with the magazine's ideal conception of a society where the real demands of consumers determined the nature of production. Activists like Warne, Kallet, Palmer, or Dr. Harold Aaron interpreted prohibition as a foolish and repressive experiment that denied consumers their freedom of choice as it increased the price and decreased the availability of tobacco. Heywood Broun, an early member of the Consumers Union board, wrote of the absurdity of modifying patterns of smoking by ignoring them. "The notion of the suppressors," he wrote, was that "if a thing is never mentioned it will cease to exist."[18]

The staff never entertained the possibility of promoting a return to prohibition, but it needed to decide whether to treat cigarettes as commodities to be rated in relation to their quality, or as symptoms of an undesirable social problem. Their experience in testing liquor had taught the workers that many subscribers held ethical and religious objections to indulgence. Arguing in 1937 that liquor should be rated "unacceptable" or not rated at all, readers protested the first "Report on Alcoholic Beverages" in numbers large enough to cause the board to postpone another until a canvass could be taken of the membership. Regardless of the superiority of one brand of Scotch to another, a reader wrote, the magazine damaged the consumer interest by conferring respectability on the habit. Rating cigarettes threatened to raise similar objections.[19]

While in 1936 the medical evidence about the risks of smoking remained inconclusive, no one outside the tobacco industry suggested that the product was healthful. For unemployed and poverty-stricken workers of the depression, cigarettes, it could be argued, constituted an unnecessary expense. Indeed, the magazine considered rating every cigarette "unacceptable," and at the annual meeting in 1937 the members debated limiting coverage of smoking to helpful information about how to quit or cut down.

Yet assuming an immediate antismoking position would have conflicted with a vision of consumer sovereignty to which the magazine and consumer advocates tried to adhere. Convinced that much of the huge demand for cigarettes had been induced by manipulative advertising, Warne and Kallet believed that the movement had an obligation to respect and analyze "misguided" consumption patterns of the public, even as it tried to change them "by providing guidance in the selection of channels of expenditure and a knowledge of essential facts with respect to commodities." With respect to cigarettes, *Consumer Reports* explained that those who advocated prohibition or temperance "would have small hope of fighting against the current" until conditions in the dominant culture had changed drastically.[20]

Considering its commitment at once to a democratic movement and a scientific method, Consumers Union found it difficult to offer dogmatic advice on the basis of flimsy evidence. The organization sought a reputation as an educational group that used its expertise and resources to inform consumers about otherwise unforeseeable social and technological problems. That reputation conflicted with an image of a paternal organization whose questionable claim to superior knowledge justified its resort to proscriptive solutions. "Private organizations offering help in an impersonal way are less obnoxious than the idea of government interference," economist Edith Ayres at the University of Chicago had written. ". . . But we tend to be suspicious of them. Are they perhaps trying to make us want fewer things, we think, are they encouraging regimentation and forced simplicity?"[21]

The spirit of the magazine conformed to the implications of that statement. The journal would present the facts its editors and their staff developed; readers were free to draw their own conclusions from the data and to act as they chose. Therefore the magazine presented a range of theoretical and practical options whenever it could. Those options often appeared as numbers in the tables and charts that filled the magazine. Matrices containing specifications and test findings bore witness to the truth that no single recommendation suited everyone. Unfortunately, those charts and displays also left *Consumer Reports* free to conduct tests without explicitly confronting the meaning of the results in print. When the staff worried that its opinions were subjective or without a completely scientific foundation, it could hedge by presenting apparently conclusive findings in a table and then disclaiming their significance in the text. In 1938 no one knew what levels of nicotine were dangerous or how significant the differences between brands were. Nevertheless the magazine printed a full page of data about the nicotine in each brand and thereby implied that the information was important.[22]

Whether or not significant distinctions between the brands existed, the view prevailed that it would be a tactical mistake not to look for them. Members of the board felt that to suggest abstinence as the only course minimized the utility of the report. Simply to condemn the habit would confine the possible applications of product testing and consequently the possibilities for educating consumers. A proscriptive approach would have limited Consumers Union to testing smoking "remedies" or surrogates for cigarettes like cigars or pipes. The net effect might have been to deprive the report of its general interest and its impact on confirmed cigarette smokers who wanted to continue and needed guidance.

Aaron, Kallet, and Kallet's assistant Madeline Ross did not know whether the differences between brands merited discussion in terms of their quality or harmfulness, but they assumed that variations in price alone justified a comparative study. The greatest controversy within the tobacco industry and among smokers throughout the Depression concerned the appearance of inexpensive ten-cent brands, some of them made under union contract, to challenge the better-known packages. If the low-priced cigarettes equaled the name brands in quality, the magazine, by reporting that fact, might help readers to save money. Conscious of the uncertainty about health risks in smoking and of the futility of moralism about tobacco, the officers of Consumers Union decided to approach the subject neutrally. *Consumer Reports* would ask whether differences in the price of cigarettes could be justified by differences in quality, and treat the testing of cigarettes the way it treated the testing of such products as liquor, constipation remedies, or contraceptives. Making every effort to divest those goods of the special degrees of confusion invested in them by advertising and folklore, the magazine hoped to show that it could apply a general product-testing technique to commodities that advertising approached as matters of highly subjective, personal choice.

In early 1937, Arthur Kallet authorized a cigarette report that involved a medical consultant, a firm of consulting laboratory analysts, and members of the magazine staff. Dr. Harold Aaron, Kallet's medical consultant and personal friend, searched available medical literature for current opinion about the relation between cigarettes and health. Technical Supervisor Dewey Palmer arranged with a chemical laboratory to analyze thirty-eight brands to discover differences in their nicotine content, tobacco quality, and processing techniques. Madeline Ross, a chemist and later assistant technical director, devised blindfold tests to discover whether any significant differences of taste existed that could justify the divergent advertising claims of major brands. The editors meanwhile explored the economic background and labor history of the tobacco business.[23]

The July and August 1938 issues of *Consumer Reports* carried a fourteen-page discussion of the cigarette industry. Predicting that ordinary cigarette smokers probably would remain loyal to one brand of cigarettes no matter what results the magazine presented, Consumers Union advised that "if you are not too susceptible to the hypnosis of advertising, you will probably try some other brands and will change to a cheaper one that is really 'just as good.'" Without condemning the habit of smoking, the editors emphasized their central finding that the uniformity of quality, content, and taste of cigarettes betrayed the efforts of the industry to create brand allegiances. "Particular People" might prefer Pall Mall, or tired people get "a lift from Camels," but beyond the appeal of advertising jingles there appeared to be no basis for choosing one brand instead of another. The editors confessed that they could make only four points with certainty: that differences among the various brands of any type of cigarette were very small; that smoking probably was "slightly deleterious" to humans; that none of the advertised brands contained more nicotine and therefore appeared more harmful than any other; and that consequently it made sense to select the cheapest available brand of union-made cigarettes.[24]

To promote the position that "the consumer and the worker are the same person . . . who must carefully guard his interests," the editors presented a separate section about labor conditions. Combining statistics from the *Monthly Labor Review* and reports of the Federal Emergency Relief Administration and the Tobacco Worker's International Union, Consumers Union summarized its conclusions in the words of the International Labor News Service:

The Big Four [R. J. Reynolds, American Tobacco, Liggett & Myers, P. Lorillard] prosper when the country has good times; and prosper more when the country is bogged in the mire of

depression. . . . Their labor policy varies between bad and
worse. . . . [Their] social policy is transplanted from the Dark
Ages.

As a practical way for consumers to support labor, the staff recommended
twelve less familiar brands that were manufactured under union contracts
and sold at standard prices.[25]

Consumer Reports deemphasized the potential physical damage that
smoking inflicted. The journal reported the views of a Harvard phar-
macologist, Dr. Walter Mendenhall, who wrote that scientific evidence
had not established a relationship between smoking and life expectancy.
Challenging the recent finding of Dr. Raymond Pearl at Johns Hopkins
University that smokers had shorter life spans on the average than nonsmokers, the article explained that many doctors believed the difference
arose from physical and emotional factors that encouraged smoking in the
first place. Nonsmokers well might have self-protective styles of living,
the magazine suggested.

While minimizing the reliability of studies that suggested dangers to
health, *Consumer Reports* published the first tables available to the
public designating by brand the approximate proportions of nicotine in
smoke. Consulting the medical literature, Dr. Aaron had found that a
consensus among doctors identified nicotine as the chief dangerous con-
stituent. Since nicotine, as the article observed, was a common garden
pesticide and a definite human poison, "you might as well absorb as little
as possible in whatever smoking you feel obliged to do." *Consumer Reports* also listed other toxic substances that tobacco contained including
"carbon monoxide, ammonia, pyridine, prussic acid, wood alcohol, col-
lidine, formaldehyde, tars, lead and arsenic." For alert readers that list
undoubtedly must have created a presumption of danger. Aaron summarized that smoking posed "a risk of unknown magnitude."

Nicotine did not bear the same relation to cigarettes that lead residues bore to fruits and vegetables, or that leaded gasoline bore to automobiles: lead could be eliminated from fruit without ruining its flavor, but
smokers received their basic satisfaction from elements that allegedly
were the most dangerous. If conclusive documentation existed about the
harm of smoking, *Consumer Reports* might have been more forthright
about discouraging consumption, but in the light of the relationship between the satisfaction of smoking and the risk, the magazine continued to
stress the chaos and inefficiency that resulted from a marketplace where
product information came only from producers:

Cigarette advertising, fighting hard to deny this sameness [of all
cigarettes], is generally misleading, often false, and most of the

time laughable. Space forbids an analysis of the claims made by ardent copywriters, vaunting the toasting, the coughlessness, the satisfaction, the costly tobaccos, the healthfulness, the bottled sunlight of various brands. Advertising agents can put a lot of enthusiasm into their praises of cigarettes. They love them. Because cigarettes charge a larger proportion of their cost price to advertising than any other commodity except cosmetics.

The cumulative effect of the article was to emphasize the uniformity of cigarettes, the deceit in their advertising, and the concentration of the industry. *Consumer Reports* looked to its readers, the press, and the government to exploit the information it provided.

The direct influence of a young, reformist magazine with a subscription list of about forty thousand readers was small. But as a longtime contributor to the magazine reflected, even early in its history *Consumer Reports* gave bureaucrats and editors of other periodicals the tools and courage necessary to tackle controversial subjects. The magazine brought technically complex problems into wider circles of debate by presenting new aspects of those problems and new ways of demonstrating them to the public. In the case of cigarettes, Consumers Union did so by publicizing scientific tests that demonstrated how advertising drew marginal distinctions between products.[26]

The cigarette report appeared while the Temporary National Economic Committee (TNEC) in Washington was holding hearings to review the concentration of American industry. Under the direction of Assistant Attorney General Thurmond Arnold, the Anti-Trust Division of the Department of Justice had begun to act in support of the TNEC by bringing charges under the Sherman Act against major firms. Among those indicted were the "Big Four" tobacco manufacturers, who stood accused of conspiracy to maintain low prices for tobacco at auction and high prices for cigarettes at retail, and with forcing farmers and retailers to discriminate against the manufacturers of ten-cent cigarettes. By 1931, the "Big Four" controlled 98 percent of the market for cigarettes, a market that did not collapse with the onset of the Depression.[27]

Officials at the Department of Justice believed that Consumers Union's findings about the similarity of brands supported their charges that advertising served primarily as a barrier to prevent smaller firms from capturing a share of the market. The department invited Consumers Union to send a member of the staff to testify. In the autumn of 1941, Madeline Ross explained in court that Consumers Union had erased cigarette trademarks from thirty-eight brands to discover if smokers could tell them apart. The blindfold tests, she said, indicated that most people

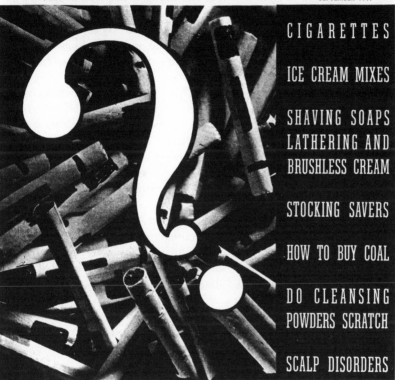

3.4   Cover, *Consumer Reports*, September 1941. Courtesy of Consumers Union.

could not spot their own brands after years of loyalty. "On the whole," she stated, "the results of the identification came out no better than the law of chance."[28]

The verdict in the lawsuit validated the case against the industry that *Consumer Reports* had argued earlier. The decision, one of Thurmond Arnold's victories, found three of the "Big Four" guilty on all counts of conspiring to monopolize every stage of the manufacturing process.

While the legal victory concerned price conspiracy, the blindfold tests and other evidence, according to *Business Week,* created "the widespread impression that what was involved . . . was that massive advertising was monopolistic and hence illegal."[29]

The TNEC inquests into monopoly in the late 1930s left the large tobacco manufacturers temporarily insecure about the future of administered cigarette prices and of unsupported advertising claims. The penalties imposed by the court were small, but the hearings contributed to the body of information that critics of the industry and of the habit would refer to in the future. Fewer than a dozen people at CU had devised, conducted, and composed the tests. The original report reached barely eighty thousand people, but the magazine managed to uncover vulnerabilities and to drive a wedge into the industry that other critics used to greater effect.[30]

Accustomed to less scientific modes of persuasion than *Consumer Reports, Reader's Digest* magazine took advantage of the scientific results that the government and Consumers Union provided. DeWitt and Lila (Bell) Wallace, editors of *Reader's Digest,* often used the magazine to crusade against tobacco. Sustained by their religious principles and lifelong antismoking education, the Wallaces regularly published articles like the 1937 testimonial of former boxing champion Gene Tunney, titled "Nicotine Knockout, or the Slow Count":

> No one has ever denied that nicotine is a poison . . . a drop of it
> on a shaved rabbit causes immediate convulsions and death. . . .
> Whenever I see a chain smoker in action I know at once that he
> is plain *sick* and should submit to a searching examination to
> discover the underlying cause of his smoking.

The tobacco industry found the *Digest* attacks irritating, especially since it accepted no advertising and, as *Business Week* wrote, "aspires to the white mantle of impartiality." Most of the tobacco industry had learned to endure the "tirades" of *Reader's Digest* in silence, despite the magazine's wide circulation of more than five million readers.[31]

Reader's Digest published a different kind of antismoking article in July 1942. "Cigarette Ad Fact and Fiction" by Robert Littell presented the results of laboratory analysis commissioned by the *Digest* several months earlier—analysis of tests practically identical to those Consumers Union performed in 1938. Measuring the nicotine content of seven leading brands, the *Digest* found them alike in every respect. Referring to the blindfold tests that Consumers Union presented to the Department of Justice, the article concluded, as Consumers Union had, that differences in nicotine and other qualities among the brands were small. No single brand was "so superior to its competitors as to justify its selection on the grounds that it is less harmful."[32]

That conclusion provoked the cigarette industry to break its customary silence and charge *Reader's Digest* with "inadequate research" and with using "poor sampling techniques." One manufacturer, however, found the product-testing approach a boon to its sales. The *Digest* report had given the top-listed cigarette a chance to boast of its "superiority." P. Lorillard embarked on a major advertising campaign announcing that Old Golds had been found "lowest in nicotine, lowest in throat-irritating tars and resins, as shown . . . by unsolicited, independent tests . . . made for *Reader's Digest*." *Consumer Reports* reviewed those developments with tempered satisfaction:

> Anyone who will get out the facts is doing a much needed service, and the more who will do it the better. Congratulations, *Reader's Digest*. Move over, CU. . . . But the *Digest* had hardly hit the stands before Old Gold was in the papers with an advertising campaign urging the citizens to get a copy of this "highly respected magazine" and see how well Old Gold fared.
>
> We think it should have refused to let Old Gold prostitute its findings, as we refuse to let advertisers prostitute ours. Since it apparently didn't, only the expected happened.[33]

On its own, *Reader's Digest* complained to the Federal Trade Commission (FTC). The Wheeler-Lea Act of 1938 provided the commission with authority to investigate false and misleading advertising, but, until pushed by the *Digest*, it did not wade into the morass of hyperbole about cigarettes. So many violations of the codes filled the print media and the airwaves that the public might have considered action against individual advertisements capricious and futile. In 1942, however, the commission took action. It brought suit against Camel and Philip Morris in August; against Old Gold in April; and against Lucky Strike, Camel, and Chesterfield in September. In the course of the next decade, the FTC proceeded against almost every major tobacco company at least once—

> against the claims of Camel that it aided digestion, relieved fatigue and never irritated the throat; against the claim for Pall Mall that it filtered the smoke in such a way as to get rid of throat irritants; against the claim for Philip Morris that it was less irritating to the upper respiratory tract; against the claims for Lucky Strike that "with independent experts . . . it's Luckies

2 to 1"; against the claim for Kool that it gave protection against colds.

Citing the *Reader's Digest* tests and its own investigations to prove the deception involved in the advertising of P. Lorillard, the Federal Trade Commission won its case against Old Gold in 1943. The FTC forced the company to discontinue that line of advertising, but its victory was limited. Once Old Gold stopped referring to the *Digest* results, Avalon cigarettes started to advertise alone similar lines. The incapacity of the FTC to police cigarette advertising became obvious as the number of complaints increased. The commission acknowledged that "by the time a complaint took effect, the objectionable advertising had generally been retired from over-use." Launching complaints on an individual basis appeared fruitless, but the commission had no better alternative.[34]

If the FTC could not keep tobacco advertising "honest," it was able to focus censure on the industry. Both the attempts and the failures of the commission illustrated and reinforced the indictment by Consumers Union. Pressing the government to regulate the quality of information about consumer products, and encouraging stronger governmental authority to ensure minimum standards and maximum competition, the magazine constantly expressed its general concern about the manipulation of consumers.

Verification of the Danger
of Smoking

The fervor that had characterized the earlier crusades against tobacco left the workers at *Consumer Reports* skeptical about connecting smoking to disease. "If you believed the Henry Ford generation," one member of the staff recalled, "smoking was responsible for all the ills known to man." Dismissing that possibility, Consumers Union after 1938 extended its preferred kind of analysis and rated pipe tobacco and cigars according to taste, cigarette lighters according to their durability, and, in the midst of the cigarette "famine" of 1945, even offered advice about "rolling your own." After the war, however, Consumers Union responded to a prospering economy, a national readership, and a conservative political climate. The organization converted several of its earlier economic arguments into the language of scientific concern for public health and became sensitive to the social cost of smoking.[35]

The "Health and Medicine" section of *Consumer Reports* rapidly expanded until, by 1948, it consisted of six or seven pages in each issue.

Aaron expanded the Medical Advisory Board, adding Walter Alvarez of the Mayo Clinic and Marion Sulzberger, an eminent dermatologist. Articles about child rearing and children's diseases; about national medical insurance and the need for control of the advertising of nonprescription drugs; about polio vaccination and the advantages of community fluoridation diverged from a product-testing format to offer general advice about the consumption of medical services. Throughout the magazine, tests of commodities like pesticides, work-tools, food, and home furnishings paid growing attention to potential hazards to safety and health. Except for ratings of automobiles, the discussions in "Health and Medicine" between 1945 and 1955 proved to hold more interest for readers than any other feature in *Consumer Reports*.[36]

Dr. Aaron's involvement with "Health and Medicine" led him into the debate about smoking in the community of medical research. At the close of the 1930s, medical journals began to print studies that implied that smoking might be responsible for serious illness in otherwise healthy people. Dr. Raymond Pearl, a pioneer in American biostatistics, published a landmark study in 1938 which concluded that smoking unquestionably brought with it a reduction in life span, and that the degree of reduction related directly to the amount of tobacco people used. His study for the first time verified in statistical terms the standing assertion of the moralist antismokers that the longevity of the general population suffered because of cigarettes. The next year a German study compared habits of persons with and without lung cancer and suggested a strong relation between the disease and cigarettes. Also in 1939, Dr. Alton Ochsner, a respected New Orleans surgeon, contended that the increase in pulmonary carcinoma was "due largely to the increase in smoking, particularly cigarette smoking." Cardiovascular diseases also caused concern. Dr. H. J. Johnson reported in 1940 that after examining 2,400 electrocardiograms of males who apparently were healthy, he discovered 50 percent more distorted or diseased coronary patterns among smokers than among nonsmokers.[37]

By 1944 more than six reputable studies pointed in the direction of a relationship between cigarettes and cancer. The managing director of the American Cancer Society (later to become head of the Tobacco Industry Research Committee), Dr. Clarence Cook Little, reported that "although no definite evidence exists concerning the use of tobacco and the incidence of lung cancer, it would seem unwise to fill the lungs repeatedly with a suspension of fine particles of tobacco. . . ."[38]

From 1930 to 1948, the rate of death among white males in the United States as a result of bronchogenic (lung) cancer increased by 411 percent. It became apparent to researchers that lung cancer had reached

epidemic proportions. Research undeniably was scattered and preliminary, but cigarettes had become prominent suspects in the search for an
answer to the rising incidence of cancer and heart disease.[39]

Like other doctors who smoked, Aaron tried during 1946, 1947, and
1948 to weigh the satisfaction that smoking gave him against the mounting
statistical evidence that it endangered his own health. Aaron's friend Dr.
Morton Levin, a pioneer in the epidemiology of lung cancer, alerted him
to the emerging signs of a connection between cigarettes and cancer, and
between cigarettes and cardiovascular diseases. Were cigarettes "inher-
ently" dangerous? Could they be made more safe? Medical reports implied that nicotine was the primary dangerous ingredient in smoke and
that cigarettes lowest in nicotine might be safest. Scientists, however, did
not know whether nicotine actually caused the ill effects attributed to it.[40]

As medical evidence accumulated, Aaron found reason to temper his
criticism of the moralist tradition. He began to write about the research
that had been done and work that needed to be done. Asking whether
people with heart disease could smoke safely, in the March 1948 issue of
Consumer Reports he analyzed a Columbia University study which found
that "the great majority" of people with coronary artery disease could
smoke "in moderation" without worry, but that "moderation" could only
be defined in consultation with doctors. The medical community since
the 1930s knew that people with peculiar circulatory problems developed
blood clots in their fingers or toes as a result of smoking; extreme cases
required amputation. For these and other people with certain heart diseases, Aaron wrote, smoking was dangerous.[41]

With the help of Irving Michelson in the Chemical Division, Aaron
addressed commercial and medical developments in the smoking controversy in January 1949. He explored the new, low-nicotine John Alden
cigarettes and pipe tobacco. The Consumers Union taste-testing panel
judged them foul and unsatisfying, but the redeeming feature of John
Aldens lay in their containing one-tenth the nicotine of other brands.
Aaron assured readers that moderate smoking had "no substantial immediate effects on *most* people," but reminded readers that several diseases were "definitely made worse by smoking." *Consumer Reports* for
the first time alluded to a tradition of opposition to smoking and called for
continued research to discover how harmful cigarettes really were:

> The "coffin-nail" literature of the anti-cigarette leagues pub-
> lished stories of how two drops of nicotine on the tongue of a cat
> would kill the animal in two minutes flat, how a canary was once
> killed by holding a drop of nicotine too close to its bill; and how a
> soldier in World War I . . . committed suicide by eating a

package of cigarettes. Thousands of more scientific studies have been published since then . . . but many of them either used too few participants to be decisive, or were concerned with defending the industry . . . or were pervaded with a moralistic anti-cigarette bias.

From a medical instead of a moral perspective, the discouragement of smoking might make sense; but without more medical data, Consumers Union would not make positive recommendations. Aaron suggested moderation or John Aldens—if an addicted smoker could tolerate either.[42]

Medical inquiries into the relationship of smoking to disease became more frequent. In 1950, Drs. Ernest Wynder and Evarts Graham of Washington University investigated the smoking habits of 605 men with cancer of the lung and found 96.5 percent of them had smoked at least half a pack a day for twenty years, and that only eight had been nonsmokers. Drs. Richard Doll and Bradford Hill reinforced those findings with the results of a London study published in 1952. Comparing the habits of 709 hospitalized lung cancer patients with the same number of patients of the same age and sex who did not have cancer, Doll and Hill found smoking to be the most important difference between the groups.[43]

Those studies were "retrospective," conducted by doctors questioning patients to discover the possible antecedent causes for their disease. Members of the industry and several well-known scientists contended that bias might enter a study whenever a patient tried to account for his own illness. To meet methodological criticism and to discover other possible effects of smoking, the first large "prospective" studies—following a health population forward in time—began in England and the United States in 1952.[44]

The findings of the medical community began to reach a wider public audience through reports in the religious press and *Reader's Digest*. In late 1953 the results of a study conducted by Drs. Wynder and Graham at the Sloan-Kettering Institute became public; cancer could be induced on the skin of mice by tobacco-tar condensates. A significant step in tying tobacco tars to the development of cancer, this study resembled the experiment that Mussey performed with cats in 1833, at least in the way its results could be reported in a graphic and arresting way that captured the essence of the problem.[45]

Roy Norr, a public relations expert who had directed the campagin against reaching "for a Lucky instead of a sweet" for the candy industry, interviewed Dr. Wynder for the *Christian Herald* late in 1952. He wrote an article that *Reader's Digest* condensed into "Cancer by the Carton," a two-page summary of recent research which, as Norr himself put it, "crashed the smoke barrier and brought the problem for the first time to the attention of many millions of people." *Time, Life,* the *New Republic, Colliers, Newsweek,* radio, and newsprint media all picked up the news. "Until the Wynder-Graham report," wrote *Life,* it could not be stated that any cigarette ingredient could cause cancer in a living creature." Now it could. Taken by surprise, the tobacco industry through its trade publication *Tobacco Leaf* could only explain that these "attacks" were addressed to the "medical, social and religious animosities and prejudices of the country," that the "moribund alcohol-obsessed temperance movement" had "taken them to its bosom as something extremely touching." To offset the adverse publicity and the ensuing decline in sales that the industry began to encounter, cigarette manufacturers began to develop a campaign against what they called "the health scare."[46]

The response of the industry to the "health scare" involved two initiatives. In a full-page advertisement in 448 newspapers, four of the five major producers announced the creation of the Tobacco Industry Research Committee (TIRC), whose function would be to investigate the relation of tobacco to health. *Consumer Reports* suggested that in some respects this resembled "burglar-financed research into the perfection of a crack-proof safe," but recalled that the industry did have a vital interest in the development of a harmless cigarette. Directed by Dr. Clarence Cook Little, the TIRC would fund basic research and issue annual reports. Year after year, those reports advised against "hasty conclusions" about any relationship between cancer and smoking:

> Any possible role of smoking in the etiology of lung cancer
> remains an unresolved question . . . so many unknowns still
> obscure the whole field of cancer causation that it is not possible
> at this stage to say either "this is it," or "this is not it," about any
> single factor.

From 1954 until 1963, that stance remained the basic position of the TIRC.[47]

Manufacturers also geared their response to the faltering market for cigarettes. Public confidence in the safety of cigarettes was low even before the release of the medical studies. A Gallup poll discovered in 1949 that 52 percent of smokers thought their habit dangerous and had attempted to give it up. Throughout 1954, sales dipped below their 1953 levels, the first decline since the Depression.[48]

To assure the public that tobacco products had been changed to confront the possible peril to health, the industry developed filter-tip and king-size cigarettes. The advertising for these brands suggested that filters or longer cigarette butts were eliminating or transforming the irritating components of smoke. Between 1952 and 1954, the share of the total market that filters and king-size blends occupied increased from 18.3 to 36.7 percent.[49]

The efforts of the Federal Trade Commission to police the claims of health protection did not inhibit the industry's advertising. As *Consumer Reports* stated, "No copywriter worth his Brooks Brothers suit would let an FTC order stop him from using health appeals if he felt they would be effective." In 1952 the industry spent sixty million dollars on advertising about the rewards of smoking. Lucky Strike claimed to be "clean." Kent suggested that "for the first time ever," smokers could get "real health protection." Pall Malls would "guard against throat scratch." Old Gold promised "a treat instead of a treatment." By the end of 1955, sales were approaching their pre-scare levels and heading upward.[50]

Kallet, Aaron, Michelson, and Dexter Masters, who was in charge of the editorial staff, studied the events surrounding the release of the Wynder studies. They noticed that while the press and electronic media paid some attention to scientific detail, that coverage did not suggest how confirmed smokers should make sense of the new findings or new developments in the industry. The cautious journalism that most magazines provided would not shake confidence in the industry for long, especially in the face of the increased volume of advertising. Despite the fact that a book called *How to Stop Smoking* made its way toward the best-seller lists, Michelson, Masters, and other workers at *Consumer Reports* knew that the mere exposure of smoking as a collective problem would not necessarily change the behavior of individuals.[51]

In 1952, the planning committee and the board of directors authorized more intensive study of the cigarette industry than ever before. Kallet, Aaron, and Masters, along with Morris Kaplan (technical director), Mildred Brady (editorial), and Irving Michelson (chemistry), worked out an approach to the problem that would capitalize on the previous work of the organization, but, as in 1938, the staff divided into two groups: those who wanted to condemn the entire habit, and those who believed that the differences between brands merited rating them according to their tar and nicotine content. Kaplan and Brady believed that any rating fostered the general impression that there was such a thing as a "safe" cigarette. They asserted that smoking was a generic risk whose consequences obviated the usefulness of a product-testing approach and deserved to be discussed in general terms or else not at all.[52]

Michelson, Masters, and perhaps Aaron believed that available evidence pointed to the conclusion that "less" was better from a health standpoint: that smokers should be advised to smoke those cigarettes containing the least tar and nicotine "if they insisted on smoking," and that by rating cigarettes Consumers Union might entice the industry to compete to reduce levels of tar and nicotine instead of competing on such intangible grounds as "smoothness" or "pleasurability." Most important, the protesting group believed that instead of giving consumers a false sense of security, the process of urging consumers to select low-tar or low-nicotine brands would reinforce their sense of danger about the habit. Kallet and the board agreed with that analysis. Assigned to the Chemical Division, the cigarette project proceeded.

The first well-promoted filter cigarette was Kent, manufactured by P. Lorillard Company. Developed by "researchers in atomic energy plants," and constructed with a "micronite filter," Kent claimed to remove seven times more tar and nicotine than other cigarettes. In June 1952, consultants to Consumers Union analyzed Kent and seven other brands with a smoking machine that fixed each cigarette in a glass tube and "smoked" it, leaving the results of each puff in a vial for spectrographic analysis. When it developed that Kent contained less tar and nicotine than other brands (John Alden and other low-nicotine-strain tobaccos excepted because of their poor taste), *Consumer Reports* encouraged consumers to buy Kent if they believed smoking posed a risk and yet were too attached to the habit to quit.[53]

For eleven years after 1952, *Consumer Reports* made cigarettes a major target of its criticism. No products except automobiles received such constant evaluation. Feature stories of eleven full pages or more appeared in 1953, 1955, 1957, 1958, 1960, 1961, and 1963, with many shorter reports spaced between them. Each report focused on the history of oligopoly and the structure of the market in the tobacco industry, on the evolution of the physical characteristics of cigarettes, and on the debate over the threat to health. The magazine used criticism of advertising as well as its program of testing to persuade the public of its growing conviction that cigarettes endangered health.[54]

The editors grew progressively more respectful of folk wisdom that had labeled cigarettes as "coffin-nails, gaspers, weeds, pills, lung-dusters, dopesticks and poison sausages." Aaron revised his impression of the earlier prohibitionist tradition. The moralism of the Henry Ford generation appeared, after further inspection, to border on intuitive wisdom. He supervised the discussion of the medical aspects of smoking, and several times repeated lists of diseases that smoking "probably contributed to," lists that antismokers had anticipated:

> chronic laryngitis, larynx tumors, tranquilizing effects on the
> higher nervous center, effects on the blood vessels and the

heart, eye disorders associated with spasm of the blood vessels of the retina, Buerger's and Reynaud's diseases . . .

Despite mounting evidence against the habit, however, *Consumer Reports* as late as 1957 did not suggest that everyone stop smoking:

> For anyone to argue that everyone should stop smoking because of its hazards would be highly unrealistic. Heightened nervous tension is the usual explanation given for the tobacco habit and there is much evidence to support it.

Consumer Reports left readers to decide for themselves whether the risks smoking imposed exceeded the gratification it supplied.[55]

The core of the articles continued to be tests of tar and nicotine content. Hoping to convey the impression that Consumers Union approached the issue not as a journalistic venture but as a scientific problem, the staff supplemented its presentation of research data with explanations of the intricacies of its tests.

After the program of testing began, Michelson noticed a surprising fact: many filter-tip and king-size brands contained *more* tar and nicotine than ordinary brands. In 1955, the magazine discovered that, on the average, cigarettes contained more of each substance than they had in 1953. In 1957, *Consumer Reports* discovered, the filter cigarettes trapped less tar and nicotine than the identical unfiltered brands had in 1953. Kent, for example, abandoned its "micronite" filter because it was *too* effective; smokers had complained that they only inhaled "[a] mouthful of tasteless warm air." Kent changed its manufacturing technique, and as a result the levels of tar and nicotine increased dramatically. With characteristic understatement, *Consumer Reports* contended that the results "shed some interesting light on the reaction of the tobacco industry to the charges over the past six years that cigarette smoking is a cause of cancer of the lung and other diseases."[56]

In spite of those startling findings, the magazine expected to receive less than an ordinary amount of follow-up publicity whenever it discussed cigarettes, and it was not disappointed. Opponents of tobacco had accused the press of bowing to pressure from advertisers, at least since Harold Ickes charged New York newspapers with burying the study by Pearl in 1938. The information that *Consumer Reports* generated about tar, nicotine, and falsehood in advertising trickled through to other magazines.[57]

Referring to the 1953 article, the front page of the business section of the *New York Times* noted the futility with which advertisers stressed the

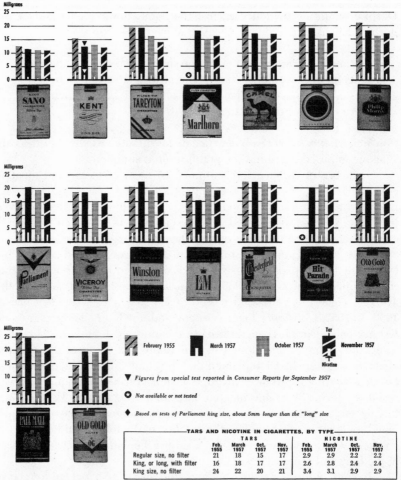

TARS AND NICOTINE IN THE SMOKE FROM 16 BRANDS OF CIGARETTES

Listed in increasing order of tar content found in CU's most recent tests; bars show averages in milligrams for smoke per cigarette (small differences, for either nicotine or tar, are of no significance).

	TARS				NICOTINE			
	Feb. 1955	March 1957	Oct. 1957	Nov. 1957	Feb. 1955	March 1957	Oct. 1957	Nov. 1957
Regular size, no filter	21	18	15	17	2.9	2.9	2.2	2.2
King, or long, with filter	16	18	17	17	2.6	2.8	2.4	2.4
King size, no filter	24	22	20	21	3.4	3.1	2.9	2.9

3.5   A graphic presentation of findings about the 1955–1957 brands, in the November 1957 issue. Courtesy of Consumers Union.

"health theme" since their reputation suffered whenever the FTC lodged complaints against them and because surveys suggested that the ads were counterproductive of sales. The *New York World Telegram* emphasized the hesitancy of the conclusions drawn by Consumers Union and ended by noting that it would be "several years before the final findings of the American Cancer Society will be determined." *Magazine Digest* reported that "the biggest news from *Consumer Reports* tests of cigarettes is that a smoker actually gets more nicotine and no less of tars from most filter tip and kingsize cigarettes . . . than from regular brands." Without mentioning brand names, Dr. Walter Alvarez syndicated the results of the Consumers Union articles in his weekly column about health to markets across the country. Seizing the 1955 report, *Top Secret* ("Hollywood-Broadway-TV-Cafe-Society-International") published a scandal headline that promised "shocking" facts that had received "no publicity in the press," facts obtained from Consumers Union, "an ivory tower, independent research organization . . . one of the country's most respected." *Advertising Age* explained that Consumers Union, "which has built a unique franchise in the product-testing field," had "trained its test-tubes on the cigarette industry" and "come up with the sensational finding that nearly all US cigarette brands actually *increased* their nicotine content during the two-year period which has seen the birth of the cancer scare."[58]

By 1957, the work Consumers Union performed with cigarettes, together with its other testing, had earned it the attention of other journalists and a larger indirect influence than it had known just five years earlier. Only *Consumer Reports* consistently had tracked the tobacco industry for a series of years, and as the indictment of cigarettes by professional health and medical associations grew stronger, the work of the magazine became more valuable to journalists and the public.[59]

After declining by some 7.3 billion cigarettes from 1953, the sales of cigarettes improved in 1955 and again in 1956, in response to the increasing sales of filter-tip brands. Vance Packard wrote in his 1957 best seller *The Hidden Persuaders* that "virtually every major tobacco marketer brought out a filter-tip brand, and in four years filter-tip sales rose 1800 percent. By 1957 the filter-tips were developing distinctive personalities, the older brands were developing more gentle personalities, and cigarette sales as a whole began trending upward again. . . ." Part of the industry believed that the "health scare" had exhausted itself. "The only certainty that has emerged," wrote *Tobacco Leaf* in that year, "is that mice shouldn't smoke."[60]

The complacency of the tobacco industry about health notwithstanding, the medical community grew certain that cigarettes were responsible for lung cancer. Three prospective studies had been initiated several years earlier and began to show results. They traced the health of 200,000 veterans holding National Service Life Insurance policies, 40,000 English physicians, and 190,000 others whose records were gathered through the efforts of the American Cancer Society. Analysis disclosed that lung cancer remained a rare disease for nonsmokers while mortality ratios among smokers were quite significant. Dr. Alexander G. Gilliam of the National Cancer Institute wrote that "it may now . . . be regarded as an established fact that white, male cigarette smokers in England and the United States suffer a substantially greater risk of cancer of the lung than nonsmokers."[61]

Scientists continued to attach great importance to environmental pollution as a cause of lung cancer, but *Consumer Reports* made the practical point that "exposure to atmospheric pollution can be controlled only by vigorous community action. Smoking, however, is a factor over which the individual can exercise personal control." After an extensive discussion in the January 1956 *Atlantic*, Dr. Charles Cammeron of the American Cancer Society summarized the case in the words of a friend, who said that if the degree of association shown to exist between cancer and smoking were to exist between cancer and, "say, spinach, no one would raise a hand against the proscription of spinach from the national diet."[62]

The Resurgence of Antismoking Advocacy

In March 1957, the Study Group on Smoking and Health, organized by the American Cancer Society, the American Heart Association, the National Cancer Institute, and the National Heart Institute concluded that "beyond a reasonable doubt . . . smoking is a causative factor in the rapidly increasing increase of . . . carcinoma of the lung." Led by the Cancer Society, those groups began broad educational efforts through schools, churches, and print media. A Gallup poll in July showed that 77 percent of the public had heard of the study group report, and that 50 percent believed that smoking caused cancer. Evaluating recent medical studies, health councils of other countries, including Britain, the Netherlands, and Denmark, began to recommend public campaigns against smoking. In the United States, politicians at first responded cautiously to appeals to become actively involved in the controversy, but public concern finally drew a response from Congress. The first congressional hearings on the subject of smoking and health took place in July 1957.[63]

John Blatnik, a Democratic congressman from Minnesota, convened his subcommittee of the Government Operations Committee for the purpose of "defining or redefining the responsibility of the Federal Trade Commission for enforcing the standards of truthfulness in advertising claims relating to the effectiveness of cigarette filters." The hearings were in fact inquests into the responsibility shown by the tobacco industry and government agencies in the face of the new evidence of risk that had become available. Blatnik scheduled testimony from officials of the Federal Trade Commission, from medical scientists, and from representatives of the tobacco industry. Among those whom the committee listened to were Surgeon General LeRoy Burney, American Cancer Society Statistician E. Cuyler Hammond, Dr. Ernest Wynder, and the director of the Tobacco Industry Research Committee, Dr. Clarence Cook Little. The committee also invited Roy Norr (now publishing a newsletter about the smoking problem) and a representative of Consumers Union.[64]

Drs. Hammond and Wynder eloquently presented the case against smoking. An official from the Department of Agriculture admitted under questioning that his agency had found that tobacco companies were substituting stronger strains of tobacco to counteract the effect of better filters, so that "essentially the consumer will get the same smoke whether he smokes regular or whether he smokes filters." The committee also heard from medical authorities uncertain about the role of smoking, including Chairman Harold Greene of the Department of Pathology at Yale, who testified that the statistical evidence presented difficulties that raised doubts about a causal connection between smoking and cancer.[65]

On the fourth day of the hearings Irving Michelson testified for Consumers Union. He offered the organization's own history of the advertising of cigarettes, called recent developments "some of the gaudiest hyperbole ever to assail a consumer's eyes and ears," and indicated several of the ways advertisers deceived the public, especially through lies of omission. Parliament brand, for one example, claimed to contain no more than one-quarter of one percent of nicotine—a fact that was true but irrelevant since it contained more of that substance than many other brands.[66]

Repeatedly the committee and gallery found Blatnik eliciting from Michelson the findings Consumers Union had gathered over the course of several years:

> *Mr. Blatnik:* Repeat that again now. Do I understand that the king-size with filter, which yields in 1957—18 milligrams of tar, gives me just as much tar, no more, no less, as a regular-size no-filter 1957 cigarette; is that correct?
>
> *Mr. Michelson:* That is absolutely correct, sir. . . .
>
> *Mr. Blatnik:* If I get this "new exclusive micronite filter," it reduces less tar and less nicotine than the original micronite filter did four years ago; is that correct? . . . [The advertising] implies that it is new and exclusive . . . but you prove that there is more tar and nicotine getting in.
>
> *Mr. Michelson:* That is absolutely correct.

Predominantly on the basis of Michelson's testimony, the committee issued a report critical of cigarette advertising, a report that concluded that the Federal Trade Commission had "failed in its statutory duty to prevent 'deceptive acts or practices' in filter-tip advertising."[67]

Since the Congress never acted on the recommendations of the Blatnik committee, the impact of the findings on the effectiveness of the Federal Trade Commission was slight. Indeed, Blatnik's subcommittee ceased to meet shortly after the close of the session of Congress then underway, a development that some congressmen attributed to the power of the tobacco industry. But the publicity surrounding the hearings tarnished the reputation of the industry and piqued public interest in the controversy.[68]

The campaign against smoking diversified after the Blatnik hearings. Working to discourage the sale of cigarettes to minors, the American Cancer Society contacted local religious and educational groups throughout the country. It lobbied at all levels of government to expand the funding for antismoking campaigns. Central to the educational effort was the attempt to keep the younger generation from beginning to smoke and the contention that it was the "duty of the Federal Government to warn boys and girls of the dangers of smoking." Consumers Union intensified its war against cigarette advertising, and called it a "triple assault on the general public": it deterred the press, radio, and TV from educational efforts, placed pressure on youngsters to begin smoking, and allayed the fears of confirmed smokers. Local chapters of the American Medical Association pressed the national organization to remove advertisements for cigarettes from the pages of its magazine and to adopt a position similar to those held by other health groups. In March 1958, the wife of a victim of lung cancer brought a suit against a cigarette company in an attempt to hold the manufacturer legally responsible for her husband's death, but that attempt and others failed after several years of litigation.[69]

In the increasingly bitter clash between the "health lobby" and the cigarette industry that occurred during 1957 and 1958, the straightforward lists of tar and nicotine content published by Consumers Union served as an objective yardstick for all parties to the debate. Warne and Masters agreed with Michelson to accelerate their testing after the hearings, and until mid-1958, *Consumer Reports* published bimonthly figures indicating changes in the brands. Warne offered the commissioner of the Federal Trade Commission the use of the facilities and personnel of Consumers Union to conduct any tests, and in February 1958 the organization joined with the tobacco industry and the FTC to standardize the scientific procedures used to determine tar and nicotine levels.[70]

By March 1958, presumably in response to the burden of publicity under which it had been operating, the tobacco industry appeared to be reducing levels of tar and nicotine. *Time* magazine reported that, according to Consumers Union, significant changes were taking place:

Burned by research linking smoking with lung cancer, and by congressional charges that many filters actually filter very little, tobaccomen are quietly reducing nicotine and tars in cigarettes. Last week *Consumer Reports*, whose March 1957 tests played a large part in the congressional blast, reported the results of the latest tests, showing milligram declines in the last year.

In April 1958, *Consumer Reports* stopped its monthly tests and recorded that, in the space of six months, eight of the major brands had reengineered their filters to transmit less tar and nicotine than previously.[71]

If the reputation of the tobacco industry had been diminished by events, the authority of Consumers Union had grown. Michelson was invited by the American Association for the Advancement of Science to deliver a talk on the subject of the responsibility of the chemist to his community. Masters and Warne appeared on television talk shows to discuss their public service projects. The ratings provided by the magazine encountered less criticism from manufacturers for lack of professional competence than earlier. Even James Bond, the daring spy created by British novelist Ian Fleming, hedged on cancer by switching from a cigarette he had smoked since his teens to "Duke of Durhams," which "the authoritative Consumers Union of America rates . . . the one with the smallest tar and nicotine content."[72]

During the last years of the decade, part of the staff began to believe that the tests of cigarettes had outlived their usefulness as well as their interest to readers. Kallet lost his position as executive director of the magazine in 1957 and, after Kallet left, Dr. Aaron contributed considerably less to the policies of the magazine. Mildred Brady, in charge of the editorial department, strongly believed that the ratings probably encouraged smokers to continue their habit. Several authorities suggested, furthermore, that if smokers reacted to weaker cigarettes by smoking more of them, no benefit to the public would result. Altering policy at least temporarily, Dexter Masters, the new executive director, decided to rate the options open to smokers who wanted to quit their habits, and to turn in the future to broad educational efforts.[73]

In 1961 Edward Brecher, for many years a free-lance writer closely associated with the magazine, came to Dexter Masters with a proposal to develop a book about the smoking problem that would present the strongest possible summary of the controversy. Masters and the board approved the proposal. After a long process of research and consultation with scientific authorities in the field and staff members of the magazine, *The Consumers Union Report on Smoking and the Public Interest* appeared in 1963 under the auspices of Consumers Union.[74]

The *CU Report on Smoking* was a 220-page product of collaboration

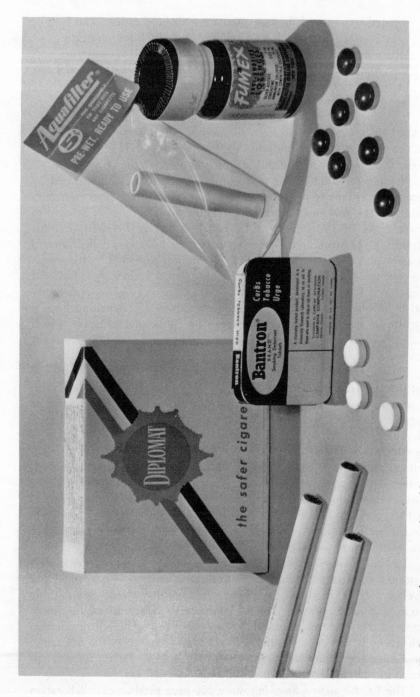

3.6 Cigarette substitutes evaluated by Consumers Union, May 1959. Courtesy of Consumers Union.

among five journalists: Edward Brecher, Ruth Brecher, Arthur Herzog, Walter Goodman, and Gerald Walker. Beginning with a summary of the medical evidence indicting cigarettes and discussing the history of the industry and the problem of cigarette advertising, the authors finally recommended seven points for a program to cope with the problem:

1. limited prohibition of sales to minors
2. the use of taxation
3. the regulation of cigarette labeling
4. the regulation or prohibition of advertising
5. a program of counter-advertising
6. a program of school education
7. a system of clinics and therapeutic aids

The book received praise from scientists, journalists, and antismoking advocates. Dr. Benjamin Spock wrote that "parents would be wise to read the *CU Report on Smoking* so that they can influence their children before it is too late." Dr. Lester Breslow, chief of preventive medicine at the California Department of Public Health, wrote that as a worker in the field he was "impressed by the meticulous correctness of language and the coherence of the report." The *New York Times* and the *New York Review of Books* found it objective, "highly important," and as William Styron wrote, "if not a joy, then at least agreeable to read." *Presbyterian Life* and *Christianity Today* suggested that while Consumers Union looked at smoking from a social and medical perspective, the religious community could "no more look at the cigarette–lung cancer problem from a morally neutral point of view than it can be oblivious to the moral implications of the daily slaughter on the highways and the human wreckage through alcoholism." The dispassionate presentation of scientific evidence spawned a new wave of moral indignation.[75]

The immediate impact of the book occurred before it actually was released. In July 1963, W. E. Hutton and Company advised that the price of stock in cigarettes remained under pressure because of the forthcoming distribution. During the same week the Tobacco Institute made public its suggestions to member companies, "urging them to avoid sponsorship of TV programs aimed at youthful audiences" and to halt advertising in college media. In an interview with the press Dexter Masters affirmed that page proofs had been sent to Dr. Clarence Cook Little before the new Tobacco Institute policy was issued and called the action "the first reaction to the book."[76]

By November, the *CU Report on Smoking* had sold more than fifty thousand copies. Other discussions of the smoking problem were also selling well. The *Wall Street Journal* printed the comment of a member of

3.7   One piece of testing apparatus for cigarettes is an assembly used in 1963 for trapping smoke solids.

the publishing industry that "the fact that they're being published at all is noteworthy." The barrier against open debate had been broken down at last.[77]

Concern about the problem of smoking and cancer mounted rapidly. Articles in major periodicals proliferated. In New York, Massachusetts, and California, groups of citizens began to work on behalf of legislation requiring warnings about the risk to health on cigarette packages and in cigarette advertising. Senator Maurine Neuberger introduced legislation in Congress to that end. LeRoy Collins, president of the National Association of Broadcasters, proposed strict codes to govern the advertising of cigarettes. Responding to inquiries from a reporter at an earlier press conference, President Kennedy in 1962 had asked Surgeon General Luther Terry to investigate the entire question. Dr. Terry chose a panel of disinterested scientists which studied the problem for six months.[78]

On the morning of January 11, 1964, the surgeon general called a press conference to release the findings of the report of his committee. At nine o'clock the committee locked the doors, distributed copies of the report, and began to announce its findings, chapter by chapter, to three hundred journalists gathered in the auditorium. Edward Brecher recalled the impact of the presentation:

> As the morning progressed you saw reporters all over that room, one by one putting out their cigarettes. At twelve o'clock I was the only one left smoking in that entire room. The doors were unlocked and everyone else dashed out for the telephones, of which a hundred had been set up.

Brecher also learned about the role that the *CU Report on Smoking* played in the work of the committee:

> Since I didn't have anywhere to dash I simply walked up to the dais to ask a couple of questions. And I hit the first member of the Surgeon General's Committee and said . . . "My name's Ed Brecher, and I am particularly interested because I did the *Consumers Union Report*." "Ed Brecher! Hey, Joe!" I was then introduced one at a time to the members of the Surgeon General's Committee, all of whom told me that . . . when they had their first meeting, the first thing that was done was that the *Consumers Union Report* was distributed . . . and they had taken off from there. . . .

The publication of the *Surgeon General's Report* initiated a new period in the effort to solve the problem of smoking. The most important medical authority in the government warned that the national addiction to cigarettes seriously threatened public health. Few adults in the nation could avoid being aware of that fact. The public had been educated.[79]

The immediate impact of the *Report* was explosive, but the problem of smoking did not vanish with one blast. The consumption of cigarettes dipped during late 1963 and early 1964, only to rise again afterward. National attention was riveted upon the problem of lung cancer for several months after the report, and then shifted to other issues. Federal legislation required manufacturers to caution smokers about the risks they took through warnings on cigarette packages and reports about tar and nicotine levels in the different brands. In 1965 a National Clearinghouse for Smoking and Health was established "to monitor the world's medical literature bearing on the health consequences of smoking," and to provide such information to the public.[80]

By the end of the decade, it had become clear that none of the steps taken had reduced significantly the dimensions of the smoking problem. As in the past, the tobacco industry responded energetically to each challenge. Marketing strategies directed toward attracting women helped to increase the number and proportion of women smokers, and the incidence of lung cancer among women rose. Despite the conclusions of health officials, the Department of Agriculture encouraged the sale of tobacco products abroad and continued to provide subsidies to farmers for growing cigarette tobacco.[81]

Consumers Union would play a less important role in antismoking advocacy after the *Surgeon General's Report*. An excellent discussion of tobacco and other addictive substances appeared in a CU special publication, *Licit and Illicit Drugs*, published in 1972, but that did not noticeably affect the debate about the regulation of cigarettes. Having decided that its testing of cigarettes had reached a useful limit, Consumers Union confined its magazine reports to summaries of legislative and political developments and to the advocacy of regulations governing the advertising of cigarettes on television. CU contributed little new evidence of its own.

The scientific approach that CU embodied had supplanted and then revived the moralistic tradition. People had been educated about the risks they encountered if they chose to smoke, and manufacturers had been encouraged to produce cigarettes that supposedly were safer than before. Part of the government had been urged to explore the relation between smoking and health. New organizations developed that were dedicated exclusively to diminishing the proportions of the national smoking habit. A great deal had been done and much remained to be done, but the problem had moved beyond the reach of Consumers Union's method.[82]

CHAPTER IV

Accidents and Injuries: Testing the Automobile Industry

MONTHS BEFORE THE publication of *Consumer Reports* began in May 1936, the board of directors of Consumers Union authorized Dewey Palmer, the technical supervisor of the organization, to study automobiles. That June the magazine published a report that compared the inexpensive 1936 model cars. Similar investigations went forward in the months and years that followed, until by 1949 *Consumer Reports* carried ratings or discussions of automotive topics nearly every month. Ratings of cars became the most popular regular feature of the magazine. In 1953 and in succeeding years, the editors supplemented their ordinary coverage with an annual issue that reviewed only cars, as a response to "the steady interest, sometimes verging on idolatry, with which millions of Americans regard their own or their neighbor's or the auto dealer's models." From the end of World War II until after 1966, Consumers Union spent more time, space, and money reporting about automobiles than about any other type of commodity.[1]

The coverage that *Consumer Reports* presented took two directions. The ratings and features were designed in part to provide readers with practical guidance. The staff therefore prepared its recommendations to reflect the taste of the public for large, powerful, attractive, and comfortable vehicles. In a broader sense, the auto testers wanted to remind the public to consider informed choice as a social responsibility. Since "sales departments and not engineers" had "sold their vision of automobiles to the public," the editors and technical consultants at Consumers Union tried to refine standards of judgment about cars to protect a larger consumer interest.[2]

75

The auto consultants looked as dispassionately as they could at automobiles. They explored fuel economy. They examined the value of different models at resale. They noted the room for baggage and the leg space for passengers. They made efforts to discover what repairs a car would need after it had been purchased. They praised technological developments that they believed were true improvements and criticized aspects of the industry that they thought were detrimental to the development of functional transportation. From the beginning, the consultants tried to determine the relative safety of cars, even though traditional proponents of traffic safety denied the relevance of vehicle design to the prevention of severe accidents. The product-testing approach of Consumers Union led it to contribute to the popularization of a concept of safety that fixed part of the responsibility for accidents and injuries on the design of cars themselves.[3]

Background: The Progressive Movement for Highway Safety

Americans welcomed the automobile when it began to appear on American streets and highways during the 1890s. Social forecasters soon predicted far-reaching and positive consequences from the new invention. Opposition to cars sometimes materialized, as when farmers in Minnesota plowed up gravel roads to prevent cars from passing over them. But the isolated nature of protest stood in contrast to widespread acceptance of motor-driven transportation, and expressions of uneasiness about the changeover from the horse to the car occurred in the context of general national approval.[4]

Beginning late in the 1890s, however, pedestrians and owners of horses expressed worry about reckless motorists and runaway vehicles. Police began to receive complaints about horses being frightened by speeding cars. To apprehend irresponsible drivers, municipal and state governments passed laws that required the registration of motor vehicles. By 1902, speed limits of eight miles per hour had been set in Savannah, San Francisco, and Cincinnati. The popular magazine *Outlook* reported in 1908 that it was "difficult to persuade the public, who find in almost every morning's paper a report of one or more automobile accidents of a serious nature, that it is as safe to drive an engine twenty to forty miles [an hour] over a highway as to drive a pair of horses eight to ten miles an hour." By 1909, thirty-four states had restricted the permissible speed of cars to twenty-five miles per hour or less.[5]

The congested traffic in cities also became troublesome and dangerous. Trolley cars, horse-drawn traffic, and motorcars crowded pedestrians off downtown streets. Outdoor business and play receded from streets to sidewalks and, in many cases, from sidewalks, indoors. More than ever the street became a conduit instead of a meeting place. Many communities began to discourage stopping or standing in roads. "A man has a right to walk in the road if he pleases," advised E. F. Saxton of the Philadelphia Bureau of Highways in 1911, "but he had better not, especially at night."[6]

The use of assembly lines to produce cars, and of new selling techniques to distribute them, led to more cars and more drivers on the road. Competition among more than a hundred manufacturers resulted in phenomenal reductions in production and selling costs. The Ford Model T especially, introduced in 1909 at a price of $950, which became $600 in 1913, came into the reach of millions of Americans. Innovations in the techniques of extending credit and in the preservation and sales of used cars further extended the market. Improvements in mechanical design allowed autos to travel at greater speeds with heavier loads, and for longer periods of time, without breakdowns. Advertising began to appeal to middle- and working-class audiences in addition to the rich. By 1914, the *New York Times* reported the estimate that there was a car for every one hundred people in the United States. Indeed, nearly two million cars were added to American roads between 1913 and 1915 alone.[7]

Responding in 1903 to the "anarchy" in city streets that had been caused by an unprecedented number of vehicles, police in New York City adopted the traffic code of William Phelps Eno. The code was designed "to facilitate traffic, prevent blockades, avoid accidents and loss of life, and diminish the loss of time and money due to the lack of rules for the regulation of street traffic." New York State also began to require licenses for chauffeurs in 1903. Other states followed suit, and conventions for yielding, passing, stopping, and parking were established in succeeding years. Louis D. Brandeis in 1911 hailed the improvement of the flow of traffic in New York as "a remarkable example of scientific management," and as evidence that rational planning might solve other difficult problems created by technological advances.[8]

In spite of improvements in the coordination of traffic and the regulation of drivers, the problems grew more severe. The separate difficulties presented by the popularity of the motorcar combined to compound the likelihood of accidents. A declining average standard of driving ability undoubtedly accompanied the growing number of drivers. The greater power and range of cars made nineteenth-century country roads increasingly hazardous and obsolescent. As motorists ventured more frequently into different cities, they found radically different traffic conventions.

Those problems and others led to a precipitous rise in the number of accidents.[9]

Although the data were not then available, it has since been estimated that approximately forty-two hundred people were killed in car accidents in 1913. Two years later, close to seven thousand people died in automobile collisions, more than had ever been recorded as dying in one year in horse-and-buggy upsets. Without ever declining from one year to the next, the absolute number of motor vehicle deaths rose by more than one thousand people per year between 1913 and 1932.[10]

Government and business officials began to take notice as the number of accidents and deaths grew and traffic congestion continued. Mayors, aldermen, and leaders of commerce conducted studies to determine the effect of traffic congestion on business. Highway builders searched for the safest ways to build roads, to position signs, and to design intersections. Insurance agents became concerned about the growing demand and apparent unprofitability of fire and collision insurance for cars. Police authorities, usually the first to arrive at the scene of accidents, worked to discover the most efficient ways to structure traffic patrols and to enforce traffic regulations. Newspaper editors started to give coverage to the growing incidence of accidents. In the face of a confused body of law that had been intended to apply to a horse-drawn system of transit, lawyers and judges tried to bring consistency to their legal settlements.[11]

Methods of improving traffic safety also began to receive the attention of industrialists and engineers as part of a growing national and international concern about the hazards created by machines. After 1909, so-called "museums of safety" were established with the help of national governments in Holland, Britain, and other European countries. Led by Elbert Gary of United States Steel, a number of American industrialists in 1911 founded an American Museum of Safety in order "to promote industrial welfare" and "to show the community just what they [industrialists] are doing to prevent accidents and promote industrial health." Like the Museum of Safety, the National Congress for Industrial Safety was organized in 1912 to demonstrate and to disseminate among workers and plant directors an awareness of the importance of industrial safety. Sponsored by businessmen and organizations, including the Red Cross, the National Congress of Parents and Teachers, and the National Consumers' League, the congress held conferences where engineers exchanged information about records of safety and techniques of accident prevention. At open sessions, speakers exhorted their audiences to enlarge their educational efforts and to recruit new members. According to Florence Kelley of the Consumers' League, the growth of the safety movement would reflect "a new value being placed on the life of the working man." By 1914 the congress had changed its name to the National Safety Council (NSC), had widened its interests to include "public" as well as industrial accident prevention, and had included the advocacy of traffic safety as one of its major tasks.[12]

The automobile industry joined the safety movement in seeking to improve the occupational environment at its assembly plants. The industry refused, however, to publicize the deficiencies of travel by automobile. "In all the history of American automobiling," asserted a municipal traffic expert in 1914, "there isn't a single instance on record in which either manufacturers or owners have contributed ideas or plans for the solution of the ever-increasing traffic difficulties." Early traffic safety councils usually operated without cooperation from manufacturers or dealers.[13]

The number of fatalities from collisions had risen to 15,300 by 1922. The National Safety Council later took comfort in the fact that deaths *per miles travelled* had declined, but it also recognized the dramatic absolute increase in the number of total injuries. *Motor* magazine in 1923 feared that the public would react to the problems of safety and congestion by altogether banning cars from some city streets. *Motor Age* referred to the deaths and injuries from automobiles as "one of the big economic problems of the day." In the face of the mounting antagonism toward the automobile, the automotive industry began in the 1920s to take a significant part in the definition of the direction of safety efforts through its leadership and through financial support given to university research efforts, safety councils, and government advisory groups.[14]

At the request of a safety movement that included state and local highway officials, policemen's groups, insurance executives, civic organizations, and also the National Highway Research Board (founded in 1920), Secretary of Commerce Herbert Hoover convened the first national conference on street and highway safety in 1924. Hoover had "talked much about the elimination of waste in industry, in dollars and sense, and in time," and he discovered in traffic accidents "a waste in human lives each year equal to one-third of the American losses by death in the World War."[15]

Conference committees investigated highway conditions, vehicle codes, driver licensing arrangements, and motor vehicles. The work of the Hoover conference soon narrowed to standardizing traffic regulations and compensating for "an almost total lack of systematic effort to secure accurate data about accidents, their types, causes and means of prevention." The conference reconvened in 1925 to initiate the first nationwide effort to gather uniform information about accidents and to draft the first model uniform vehicle code.[16]

Many groups showed great interest in preventing automobile accidents, but few safety proponents believed that the improvement of the design of cars was a promising approach to reducing collisions. The "Committee Report on the Motor Vehicle" at the Hoover conference judged that the overwhelming majority of accidents were due to "other than mechanical causes." It suggested, for example, standardizing the location of brake pedals and the improvement of visibility from the driver's seat, but it minimized the importance of such changes. A 1924 study by the National Automobile Chamber of Commerce which examined 280 automobile accidents had traced only 7 to a defect in the vehicle. The NACC and the Hoover group agreed that the preponderant causes of deaths on the highway were bad driving, unwary pedestrians, and dangerous road conditions. [17]

The mechanical shortcomings of vehicles appeared to be technical problems best left to engineers within the automobile industry. The Society of Automotive Engineers (SAE) had developed out of an informal advisory group to become an influential body whose recommendations frequently became formal standards. In the process of fostering the interchangeability of parts, the SAE encouraged numerous safety improvements. The introduction of safety glass, directional signals, inflated tires, and other modifications between 1913 and 1927 supported those who suggested that the defects of the motor vehicle would be resolved in due course. "Those cars are as safe as we engineers can make 'em; now it's up to the man at the wheel," an auto industry spokesman told the Literary Digest in 1935. There was reason to assume that, unassisted by the pressure or advice of amateurs, safety features would be integrated into new model cars as they were proven to be effective. [18]

As the safety movement continued to grow during the 1930s, its approach emphasized the moral responsibility of the driver for the protection of the passengers in his vehicle. In 1934 the Bureau of Public Roads began to prepare a study which attributed most accidents to irregular laws, inadequate vehicle inspections, and "accident-prone" drivers. The Automobile Manufacturer's Association in 1935 launched a project to encourage improved highway engineering, better enforcement of traffic laws, and improved driver education, while School Life magazine offered "Ten Commandments for Safe Driving." [19]

In summer 1935, Readers' Digest provoked considerable public alarm with the publication of a gruesome article written by J. C. Furnas, "And Sudden Death." Having an accident in modern cars, Furnas wrote, was "like going over Niagara Falls in a steel barrel full of railroad spikes." Furnas proclaimed that what the nation needed was "a vivid and sustained realization that every time you step on the throttle, death gets in

4.1 Traditional approaches to reducing accidents and fatalities emphasized the importance of remaining mentally alert. "Safety Begins Up Here," reproduced from *Safety* magazine, XI, 1925, 140.

beside . . . waiting for his chance." "And Sudden Death" reached an
estimated 35 million people through *Readers' Digest*, newspapers, and
leaflets.[20]

In the same way that many Americans blamed widespread individual
irresponsibility and moral weakness for the economic hardship of the
Depression, they appeared willing to assign guilt for the tragedy of traffic
deaths to individual acts of foolishness. A Gallup poll taken in December
1935 revealed that 70 percent of the public favored the special marking of
cars whose drivers had been at fault in accidents. On New Year's Day
1936, President Roosevelt issued a personal challenge to Americans to
consider accident prevention as a test of national fibre. The solution to
highway safety could "finally depend on all of us as motorists" to overcome
"carelessness, discourtesy and recklessness."[21]

The Driver as a Consumer

From the standpoint of consumer advocates late in the 1920s, the empha-
sis placed by safety groups on the need for greater vigilance by drivers
had to be supplemented with a concern for safety as an element of automotive performance. From that perspective, an automobile was a product, and the relative safety of any car was one important piece of
comparative product information that drivers as consumers could not
discover through conventional American marketing. Discouraging the
consumption of defective cars might lead to safer travel as it exposed
problems in the American economy and illustrated the value of product
testing.[22]

With only a million dollars, Stuart Chase and Frederick Schlink
estimated in 1927, a testing agency might run every type of car made over
a standardized road test. The results then could be analyzed and published. Information would be provided to the consuming public about the
number of failures of one kind or another after 1000 miles; about braking
ability, gasoline mileage, and other important characteristics. By promoting the purchase of more durable cars, the consumer would benefit "not
only by making the car last as long as we should want to have it around,
but . . . by reducing by a large factor the number of accidents due to
failing axles, brakes, and so forth." *Your Money's Worth* proposed that "if
you really wanted to get back of the advertising, it [product testing] would
help tremendously." Pursuing that reasoning, workers at Consumers' Research and then at Consumers Union tried to compare different makes of
cars.[23]

A chronic shortage of funds prevented Consumers' Research from conducting adequate auto tests during its first years, and Consumers Union confronted similar financial difficulties. The entire operating budget of Consumers Union during 1936–1937 amounted to only $114,000. "Of course you couldn't buy cars, there just wasn't enough money," recalled Dewey Palmer, the technical supervisor.[24]

A former physics teacher who had written about automobiles for Consumers' Research, Palmer joined Lawrence Crooks, a free-lance journalist with a degree in English from Amherst College and some experience at Yale's Sheffield School, to make technical assessments of cars for *Consumer Reports*. Without money to buy cars, the two men located reliable and impartial information as best they could. They visited showrooms, borrowed cars from their friends, and talked to other mechanics. Combining their own judgments about performance with the data that emerged from stock-car races and other published sources, they learned enough to assign grades and ranks to each model. Then they translated their findings into verbal comparisons.[25]

Safety figured importantly in their ratings. Since 1933, Palmer had argued for "Automobile Safety Before Beauty" in *Consumers' Research Bulletin*. He suggested that contrary to the publicized position of the industry that "autos have always been built as safe as engineering knowledge permitted," many injuries resulted from "the insufficient amount of technical skill going into the design of safety features." To Palmer, the angular shape of knobs and controls, the ill-considered contours of vision, and the poor quality of materials that were used for functional but concealed features demonstrated that styling took precedence over good engineering in production. More conservative than Palmer, Crooks took a sympathetic view of the problems faced by engineers inside the auto industry. But he too agreed that managers paid too little attention to promoting safety by altering design.[26]

The cover story about automobiles in the June 1936 issue of *Consumer Reports* ridiculed advertising and derided the general shoddiness of modern cars. Automobiles had been "deliberately cheapened to promote their obsolescence." The "flimsiness" of consumer models contrasted with the durability of taxicabs. *Consumer Reports* criticized Alfred Sloan of General Motors for calling on the public to accept a shorter life span for new cars. The report branded the 1936 models generally with inadequate visibility, unnecessary power, overloaded tires, and poor braking ability. It warned that "every modern car, with a body design which cuts the driver's vision for the sake of appearances, and with its powerful engine and high speed, is potentially unsafe."[27]

With separate articles discussing topics such as poor working conditions in the industry and the problem of selecting gasoline, *Consumer*

Reports spent the bulk of its space providing detailed information about twenty-two low-priced vehicles. The Graham Crusader, for example, provided excellent steering and stopping ability, but it offered poor visibility to the rear. The hydraulic braking system of the 1936 Chevrolet was judged to be defective. The low price, strong general performance, and "comparative safety at high speed" of the Ford V-8 Standard, on the other hand, enabled it to earn a rating as a "Best Buy." Essentially similar reports, except with additional tables and charts that offered more abundant comparative data, appeared frequently in the magazine over the following years.[28]

In 1938 Palmer and Crooks wrote *Millions on Wheels*, a special Consumers Union publication that gathered together the articles on automobiles in *Consumer Reports*. Providing "an invaluable guide for the 25,000,000 motorists in this country, informing them about every structural detail and functional oddity of the modern automobile," *Millions on Wheels* tried as well to link the imperfections of consumer technology with the problems of capitalist enterprise. Palmer and Crooks incorporated Veblen's theories about "pecuniary emulation" into a cultural and economic interpretation of technological change.[29]

Millions on Wheels attributed the nature of the American car to peculiar American conditions. The automobile expressed the spirit of a country with vast territory, enormous wealth in petroleum, and "a restless people eager to show by what they owned that they are coming up in the world." Because of intangible aesthetic and emotional considerations, consumers did not give sufficient attention to performance before they decided on a car: they bought cars that served psychic as well as practical needs. Manufacturers therefore chose to devote themselves to "annual style changes and functionless chrome at the expense of transportation values." Crooks and Palmer were convinced that the cause of efficient, durable, and safe transportation would be served if drivers as consumers could be educated to seek functional excellence instead of prestige when they bought, or if manufacturers could be encouraged to design cars to excel under conditions of use, instead of building them for maximum sales appeal.[30]

When Dewey Palmer resigned from his position as technical supervisor late in 1938, Kallet selected a new chief technician, while Lawrence Crooks took charge of the automotive ratings. From his home and garage in Hamden, Connecticut, Crooks, as automotive consultant for the next twenty-eight years, defined the style and approach of the automotive coverage. His nearly monthly reports—consistently the most popular in the magazine—displayed a grasp of mechanical problems, a gift for lively technical writing, and a pragmatic, conservative, common-sense approach to government regulation. Crooks emphasized the utilitarian values of automotive transport: "comfort, not luxury; economy, not top high speed; durability, not flashy performance; safety, not streamlining and deluxe fittings; [and] mechanical improvements, not gadgets." He hoped to offer "average" readers of Consumer Reports—hypothetical urban-dwelling, married workingmen who drove about ten thousand miles per year—enough information to enable them rationally to make their own comparative choices in the marketplace.[31]

Automobiles were not produced for domestic consumption between 1942 and 1946. Engaged at home in the "war against waste," Consumer Reports offered advice about storing cars for the duration, prolonging the life of rubber tires and other parts, and conserving fuel. By the end of 1945 would-be consumers were waiting with growing impatience for the renewed production of civilian vehicles. When the 1946 cars appeared, Consumer Reports struggled to find the models to rate and the personnel to help rate them. The magazine resumed its automotive ratings in May of that year.[32]

To answer new questions about cars that arose after the war, the staff refined many of its tests for comfort, safety, and general performance. It computed, for example, new indices of power, gasoline mileage, relative repair costs, and ratios of brake lining to total weight. In 1948 the organization began to purchase the cars it wanted, and to "use-test" them on the roads of central Connecticut. Crooks and his assistant would develop their technical reports, send a draft article to the editors at the main offices of the magazine, and then put the cars up for resale. In 1952 and 1953 Crooks hired additional personnel to help him out, including Fred Wood, a Yale graduate with a literary and technical background, and Joseph Ulman, an engineer with editorial skill and testing experience gained at the Massachusetts Institute of Technology and at General Motors.[33]

Consumers Union continued to take complete responsibility for the development of the ratings in Consumer Reports; it did not sign or attribute its reports to particular writers. This corporate authorship served to reinforce the reliability of the institution as a whole. But in the postwar years it added new columns of signed commentary to provide specialized and independent criticism of consumer problems. In 1947, Crooks began a signed feature called "The Auto Business" and a young architect named Eliot Noyes wrote "The Shape of Things," a series of essays intended as pleas for functional and enduring design "in distinction to the fads and false aesthetics of a merchandising culture." Noyes wrote that cars should be made beautiful only after they met requirements for "good visibility, comfortable sitting, adequate headroom, easy access to wheels for changing tires . . . and so forth." The automobile industry, he charged, had

4.2   To test the accuracy of a car's odometer, testers at CU attached a "fifth wheel" to rear bumpers. Courtesy of Consumers Union.

shown exceptionally poor aesthetic taste and questionable engineering judgment. As research into the effects of crashes became available, the insurance industry, organized civic groups, and politicians began to support the criticism CU had ventured. [34]

Safer Cars

The idea that better design might lower the number of deaths from collisions spread through segments of the engineering community following the war. Hugh DeHaven, a Canadian Air Force pilot who had survived an air collision in 1917, became interested in discovering what factors had influenced his survival. With the help of the Civil Aeronautics Administration, DeHaven established an Aeronautical Crash Injury Research Center at Cornell Medical College in 1942. That center conducted groundbreaking studies which indicated that the human body was less fragile than generally had been believed; that the "structural environment" surrounding an accident was the "dominant cause of injuries," and that the immediate environment of a collision could be modified to reduce the causes of mechanical injuries. DeHaven pioneered in the effort to eliminate sharp edges and protrusions from the cockpits and cabins of aircraft. [35]

When in 1952 the Armed Forces Epidemiological Board discovered that the services were losing more men from automobile accidents than from active duty, DeHaven transferred his experience from airplanes to automobiles and formed the Automotive Crash Injury Research Project (ACIR). At the annual meeting of the Society of Automotive Engineers in 1952, DeHaven demonstrated that people actually were injured in what Elmer Paul of the Indiana Highway Patrol had called a "second collision," a decelerative impact which occurred after an initial accident took place. Surviving accidents, he said, was a matter of cushioning people to absorb the second collision as gradually and gently as possible. It was comparable to packaging glass bottles or eggs to keep them from breaking after they fell. DeHaven convinced many people that the problem of preventing personal injuries could be confronted independently from the problem of eliminating collisions between automobiles. [36]

Work to explore the causes of injuries accelerated. Aviation crash research continued at Cornell, at Republic and Douglas Aviation, and at the U.S. Air Force Research and Development Command. By withstanding the decelerative force of thirty-five times the force of gravity in a specially controlled test sled, Air Force Colonel John Stapp demonstrated that if distributed properly the force of even the most severe crashes could be survived. Traffic safety projects that had been started at Northwestern and Pittsburgh universities expanded their scope to include the causation of injuries. Studies by John Moore and Boris Tourin at ACIR led students of accidents to realize that drivers were far safer if, after a collision, they were restrained inside instead of thrown outside a car. Investigators discovered that knobs and projections onto which passengers were thrown, even at very low speeds, caused serious injuries.[37]

Encouraged by the quickening pace of research, Crooks began to distinguish in the pages of the magazine between the effects of "first" and "second" collisions. Consumers Union in 1946 had advised drivers that safety depended on the ability of a car to avoid obstacles in its way, to stay on the road under adverse conditions, and to "absorb the forces of impact in collision or upset." In 1948 the organization declared that despite universal ignorance about which automobile body structure would best resist accidents, convertibles and station wagons were the most dangerous from the standpoint of crashes and rollovers. It found that the 1952 Hudson had a low center of gravity, good brakes, and better-than-average construction: that car appeared to have been constructed with safety in mind. But a truly safe car would not only help drivers to avoid crashes. It would protect drivers after accidents occurred:

> Passengers would be safer, especially in a crash and roll accident, if the doors stayed shut. Unfortunately, they don't. . . .
> Within the car things can sometimes go much worse than they would if designers showed more interest in safety features. Amazingly severe head injuries can result from bumps even at 20 miles per hour or less when the passenger in the "suicide" seat beside the driver jackknifes into the instrument panel of the windshield.

Letters to *Consumer Reports* from readers showed wakening interest in safety "as built into the car's behavior, as afforded by driving skill, and in terms of protection afforded by the car itself in a collision." Reflecting those interests, Consumers Union offered grants to ACIR and the National Safety Council for research into traffic safety, but those organizations declined to accept because of the "stigma" of radicalism under which Consumers Union operated. In the pages of the magazine, the auto consultants began to suggest that although manufacturers had "logical reasons (besides cost) for not constructing cars primarily on the assumption that they are going to be run into things," there were many details that required attention.[38]

When magazines, including *Time, Business Week*, and *Colliers*, after 1953 reported the work going on at ACIR, the industry took official notice of that research. The vice-president for engineering at General Motors announced the willingness of the company to extend technical cooperation. A spokesman for Chrysler's research division said that it would "cooperate in any way possible." Earle S. MacPherson of Ford stated that his company would make a careful study of the Cornell findings.[39]

Notwithstanding the pronouncements of the industry, there were few apparent safety improvements in the 1953 model cars. Consumers Union displayed its irritation with the direction in which style changes were headed. "What's Become of the Engineers?" the 1953 auto issue asked. Cars were growing longer and wider, an evolutionary trend which had "extinguished the dinosaur." Nothing was being done to keep doors from flying open in crashes. The competition to build cars of greater power and higher speed appeared to increase the chances of severe injuries when collisions occurred. No steps were being taken "to neutralize the headsmashing characteristics of dashboards, the catapulting forward of seats, the crushing of unsupported roofs." Manufacturers ignored the problems of many women and shorter drivers. The magazine concluded that "for the sake of saleable attributes, . . . features are built into cars which engineers can only be unhappy about." Supporting *Consumer Reports*, the Racine, Wisconsin, *Journal-Times* resisted the grandiose view that the curves and chrome of 1954 automobiles gave expression to the mobility and affluence of the American life-style. "The automobile is . . . first and foremost a utilitarian instrument to most of us," it wrote, "and we can afford to sacrifice some appearances for utility."[40]

The Advocacy of Restraints

The automobile industry made some efforts to improve the safety of cars in 1955. It made standard tubeless tires, sealed-beam headlights, better handling ability, and in some cases fewer knobs, hard surfaces, and projections on dashboards. Nonetheless, close to ten million automobile accidents in that year killed more than thirty-eight thousand people. That carnage disturbed many Americans. Twenty-four percent of a national Gallup survey wanted additional improvements such as wider windshield vision, better brakes, better steering, speed governors, standard directional signals, and safety belts in the new 1956 cars. Casualty insurance executives were also critical. Calculating that nearly half of all automobile insurance premiums would be returned to policyholders in 1955—almost two billion dollars—insurance men met with representatives from the major manufacturers to discuss the possibility of safer and more durable cars.[41]

Consumers Union that year repudiated the idea that the national problem of traffic deaths could be controlled by more alert or better-educated drivers. The organization declared its weariness with "fingers pointed" and "safety days and weeks" proclaimed by safety councils and automobile clubs. "Given human nature as it is and the roads as they are," the magazine wrote, "certainly the car manufacturer has some responsibility for making cars as safe and as foolproof as they reasonably can be." "Even though we may be exemplary persons most of the time, there are certain moments . . . in the lives of all of us when we become . . . emotionally off balance," the medical advisors observed in 1956. "If we happen to be driving during one of these episodes—and external circumstances favor an accident—then an accident is likely to occur." For that reason Consumers Union asked manufacturers to eliminate the "obvious and rather easily remedied safety loopholes" that remained in cars: nothing had been done to blunt the "spear pointed at the driver's heart" (the steering column), or to improve door locks. No manufacturer had made the "slightest gesture toward the installation of seat-belts, even as an extra-cost option."[42]

Persuaded by studies performed at ACIR, at other universities, and in foreign countries including Sweden and Australia, the American Medical Association in 1954 recommended to auto manufacturers that they consider the installation of seat belts in all cars. Several thousand consumers by late 1954 had in fact gone to considerable effort on their own part to locate and install belts. By late 1955, a Gallup poll revealed that 49 percent of the public favored the installation of belts in all new cars. The willingness of the industry to place seat belts in cars or to facilitate their installation became one measure of its commitment to safety.[43]

Ford and Chrysler Motors, operating in a climate increasingly hostile to the manufacturers because of highway deaths, responded positively to the growing public concern. Believing that it would be profitable to promote cars on the basis of their safety features, they prepared "safety packages" for their 1956 models, which were released in the fall of 1955. Ford presented a "Lifeguard Design" package which, in addition to making seat belts optionally available, offered other improvements:

> Energy absorbing padding was developed to protect occupants . . . similar material was incorporated in sun visors . . . a recessed-hub steering wheel was adopted to protect the driver from high-pressure contact with the rigidly supported center of the wheel. . . . Double-grip door latches were developed . . . an adhesive plastic backing was incorporated in the rear-view mirror to lower the risk of flying glass fragments when the mirror was broken . . . padded arm rests were developed, and rear-seat

retainers were strengthened to help keep seat cushions in place during a collision.

Chrysler offered similar design changes, and General Motors belatedly showed some concern about safety by promising that seat belts would be available as optional equipment on many of its models. General Motors, Studebaker, and other companies were more cautious about promoting safety; Chevrolet, for example, promised consumers that their "afternoon jaunts in the country-side" would become "shiny new adventures." But Chrysler and Ford attempted to persuade motorists to drive "safer ever after."[44]

The promotion of safety features offered Consumers Union a rationale for discussing safety in greater depth. Crooks, Ulman, Wood, and others who worked at the auto-testing facility offered strong recommendations for the modification of steering, braking, suspension, hauling, noise, vision, and engine characteristics. Consumers Union placed itself on record in favor of less elastic standards to govern the performance of cars.[45]

In the Chemical Division, Irving Michelson proposed to conduct separate tests of seat belts. Morris Kaplan, the technical director, questioned the potential interest to readers of tests that would be used mainly by the mechanics or the manufacturers who installed belts, rather than by consumers. Michelson hoped that an article that rated seat belts might impress consumers with the general importance of wearing belts, lead to stricter standards for their construction and installation, and perhaps lead customers to take safety factors more seriously into account when they bought cars. Kaplan relented. Michelson and his textile consultant developed and ran static tests—stretching, pulling, and weathering experiments—and presented a compelling argument for the principles of restraints in May 1956.[46]

Consumers Union recommended belts wholeheartedly, but it painted a sad picture of the products that were available. Of thirty-nine brands of seat belts tested, twenty-six failed because of broken stitching, webbing failures, bracket ruptures, ripped metal sleeves, or other problems. Instead of saving lives, some belts apparently created among drivers a false sense of security, or perhaps allowed positive injury in the event of an accident.[47]

News of the seat belt tests and the automotive ratings, without mention of brand names in almost all cases, circulated to the public through a limited number of newspapers and magazines in the United States and other countries. The test publicity added to the interest in seat belts generated by Congressman Kenneth Roberts (D-Ala.), who held the first

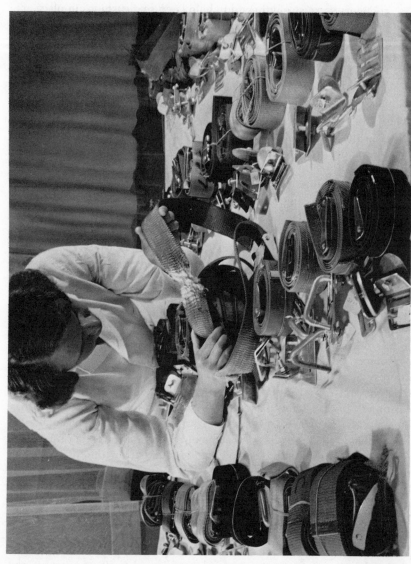

4.3. A staff member examines frayed seat belts, February 1960. Courtesy of Consumers Union.

federal hearings to consider the advisability of the universal installation of seat belts. Newspapers, including the *New York Times*, reported that seat belts were "taking hold" throughout the country. "There is no doubt that in next year's lines more of them will be utilized as never before," the paper reported. Journalistic optimism about the future of safety devices ran high.[48]

Predictions about the popularity of safer cars unfortunately were mistakenly bright. Ford and Chrysler cars sold poorly in 1956, and much of the trade interpreted the promotion of safety as the cause. The vice-president of Ford, Robert McNamara, did report in February 1957 that more than four hundred thousand seat belts had been sold, and that no other optional equipment ever gained such quick popularity. Nevertheless, the quip that "Ford sold safety while Chevy sold cars" became a common response of industry spokesmen to requests for greater attention or resources devoted to safety publicity and research. The prevalent view of executives was that to remind consumers about a safety factor was to lead customers to expect all cars to be accident-prone.[49]

While seat belts continued to be available as optional equipment in most new cars, Ford and Chrysler stopped their advertising appeals based on safety in mid-1956. The seat belt industry, which had grown rapidly that year, declined: of more than 125 firms that had been manufacturing belts, only a few survived into 1957. Safety design research continued, but without high priority or enthusiasm on the part of the industry.[50]

The popular view that the safety campaigns of 1956 had failed drove safety advocates into retreat. *Consumer Reports* briefly allowed that instead of imposing unwanted devices at additional cost to consumers, the most feasible approach to the reduction of highway deaths might be to improve the quality of driving and the condition of highways. Ratings of seat belts were discontinued because the seat belt industry stagnated. The organization in late 1956 was confused and divided about whether vehicle design was crucial to highway safety, whether the government should play a role in the establishment of safety standards, and whether the automobile industry was responding in good faith to recent research about safety. The staff could reach no internal agreement about the proper course to pursue.[51]

The mechanical evaluations of automobiles by Crooks and his staff were achieving greater sophistication and professionalism. After the middle 1950s, Consumers Union not only published more comprehensive information about cars than any magazine outside the trade press, but it developed complex statistical techniques with which to analyze information collected from members of CU about repair records and consumer satisfaction. The offices of the test facility moved in 1953 from Crooks's garage into larger quarters, and in 1957 Consumers Union incorporated Crooks as a member of the staff rather than as a consultant. Consumers Union leased access to a racing-car track and proving ground at Lime Rock, Connecticut. The amount of money spent to test cars rose from $7,000 in 1949 to more than $80,000 by 1958.[52]

In April 1957, Consumers Union renewed its vigorous criticism of the industry. Suggesting that the public wanted "smaller, safer, less powerful, more economical cars" and fewer "dreamboats," Crooks began to emphasize economy in addition to safety. The magazine indicated its disappointment with defects in the new-model cars by creating a hypothetical hybrid model which combined the padded front-seat back of a Studebaker, the distortion-free windshield of a Chevrolet, the ventilating system of a Pontiac, the visor and dashboard padding of a Ford, and the quiet of a Cadillac. Consumers Union described an experimental safety car planned by ACIR and sponsored by Liberty-Mutual Insurance Company, and praised it for its far-reaching innovations in safety design.[53]

Crooks in 1958 began to extend his criticism beyond the pages of the magazine. He spoke about his concerns to many groups, including the Society of Automotive Engineers and the Senate hearings on antitrust and monopoly, chaired by Senator Estes Kefauver. The sagging sales of 1958 model cars, he said, reflected the preferences of potential buyers who believed that the industry had lost sight of sensible principles of design. He told the Kefauver committee that while a "wholesale building into cars of cost-raising safety devices" was unwise, he wanted "a consistent, unperfunctory and thorough cleaning-up campaign."

> Look . . . at the interior of a late model Cadillac. It has a padded dash—and [yet] presents to the driver steering wheel spokes with brutally sharp edges. Examples multiply . . .

Supporting Crooks's testimony the magazine in July 1958 published the views of Henry Dreyfuss, a prominent industrial designer, in an article called "The Car Detroit Should Be Building." European manufacturers—particularly Volkswagen—were making inroads into the American sales market by recognizing the importance of economy and simplicity. American manufacturers, on the other hand, built cars "for Jazz Age America," under the presumption that American consumers were "content to find a four-wheeled juke-box waiting for them at the curb." Dreyfuss proposed specific design modifications and asked the industry to adopt uniform standards for the new models.[54]

The magazine suggested its own list of safety improvements for new cars:

A slow-down warning light at the rear of the car.

A power steering system that could retain the road sense of manual and apply power assist only when parking.

Chassis built with side rails mounted outboard to help in side-swipes.

Roll bars in roof structures.

Collapsible steering columns.

Seat belts (by far the most important safety investment, if worn) offered as inexpensive optional equipment, with secure mountings for the belts built into the car body as standard equipment.

Positive solid mountings for seat cushions and back rests.

A latch on the front seats of two-door cars.

A driver warning device to tell if any exterior parking, headlight, tail light, brake light or directional signal had failed.

Front and rear defrosters and wipers.

Dual brake cylinders.

Consumers Union asserted that everything listed could be incorporated easily into new cars within the next few years.[55]

In the newly created Public Service Projects Department, Michelson renewed his involvement in the safety controversy. In 1958 the magazine reported that "brake fluids with all the performance virtues of orange juice" could be sold legally in thirty-five states. The magazine rated fluids in order to convince consumers to persuade legislators to draft more stringent standards. "The vast majority . . . never would be guided by what we found," Michelson recalled, since in the case of brake fluids most mechanics simply dipped into a huge drum in the back of the garage. "What our testing did in that case was to point up the need for legislation more than telling people what to buy." Michelson testified about the problem in several states. Other staff members at Consumers Union sent letters to highway and legislative authorities. Fifteen states passed new brake fluid legislation as a result, and after another series of tests, and hearings before the Roberts committee, Congress approved federal standards for brake fluid, perhaps the first federal standards that directly affected passenger cars.[56]

In 1959 Michelson hired Boris Tourin, an experienced safety expert who had left the Crash Injury Center at Cornell. Intent upon investigat-

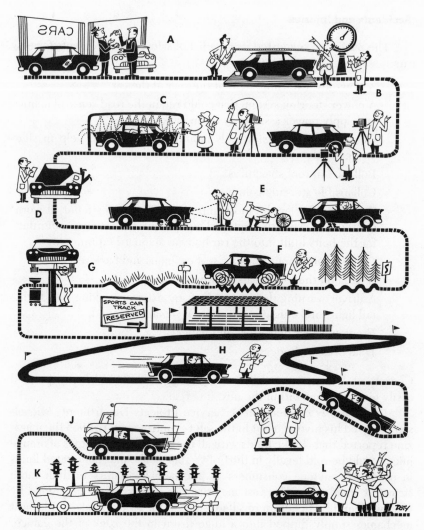

4.4 The process of testing a car in 1959. After purchase (A), a car is weighed and measured, photographed, showered, and tested for water-tightness (B,C). It is evaluated for serviceability (D), and checked for proper headlight and wheel alignment, as well as for the accuracy of its odometer (E). The car is driven over different roads at varying speeds for about 2,000 miles (F) and then re-tuned (G) before performance and economy tests are administered at a race track (H). Hill-climbing and brake capacities are measured, along with passing ability (I). Gas mileage is measured under open road and city conditions (J,K). The testers then make their evaluations, check and print their report, and trade in the car for a new one to test (L). Note that in 1959 there was no explicit place in the procedure for evaluating the safety of the car. Reproduced from the December 1959 *Guide for Small Car Buyers,* courtesy of Consumers Union.

ing accident causation "at a very basic level," the two men pioneered in the development of new ways to test seat belts and harnesses, and began to collect and organize information about vehicle design. In May 1961, they organized a Conference on Vehicle Design and Safety Research at West Point, New York, cosponsored by the Association for the Aid of Crippled Children. Representatives from the auto industry, major research projects, and government agencies presented formal papers and met for informal discussions. The proceedings were condensed into a special Consumers Union technical publication, *Passenger Car Design and Highway Safety*, released in 1962. That book became an important reference for journalists, legislators, and engineers who were interested in the problem.[57]

As a result of the West Point conference, *Consumer Reports* took stronger positions than ever before in favor of more conscientious attention to design for safety. The magazine sided with those who believed "that the most effective way to protect the motorist is to leave him as little choice as possible about installing proven safety features," and called for "the immediate and universal adoption of belts or the newer harnesses, stronger door locks, interior padding and other safety devices." In 1963 Consumers Union made a public plea for the government to sponsor a study of the relationship between car design and accident incidence. Car buyers were able to compare the price, size, and power of cars, but they had no way of knowing precisely which car was the safest. To fill that vacuum of information, Consumers Union asked for a grant "similar to those . . . which the Atomic Energy Commission and the U.S. Public Health Service have given to help CU continue and expand its fallout monitoring studies."[58]

The grant for safety studies did not materialize, however; before it could be pursued, Michelson lost a battle with the Technical Division over support for his investigations of fallout. He and Tourin left Consumers Union in 1964. The Public Service Projects Department was disbanded and its grant proposals were shelved.[59]

"Birth of a Conscience"

As the decade of the 1950s closed, public awareness of deficiencies in automotive design increased. The American Medical Association, the National Safety Council, the Public Health Service and the General Federation of Women's Clubs launched educational campaigns to encourage the use of seat belts. Paul Kearney, a journalist specializing in automotive news, published several articles questioning the safety of new cars.

Daniel Patrick Moynihan, then a legislative assistant, wrote "Epidemic on the Highways," a widely read article that considered the accelerating rate of traffic fatalities as a public health problem and called for government regulation of the auto industry. Late in 1960, CBS television broadcast a powerful documentary series, "The Great Holiday Massacre," which touched upon better vehicle design as a possible help in reducing the severity of injuries.[60]

Consumers Union encountered less resistance than ever to the reporting of its findings in major newspapers and magazines. The speeches and testimony by Crooks; the guest editorial opinions; the tests of seat belts, harnesses, children's belts, tires, and brake fluids; and the monthly automotive ratings were widely reported (without the mention of brand names). The ratings of cars earned special attention within the trade press because of their honesty and thoroughness, and more important, because of their acknowledged ability to affect the sale of automobiles. The opinions of the organization were becoming increasingly influential.[61]

The nearly one million members of Consumers Union in 1960, furthermore, had become particularly attuned to auto safety. A national poll in 1961 discovered that only 3 percent of the nation's cars were equipped with seat belts. Yet 17 percent of members of Consumers Union owned them—about five times the national average. Nearly 52 percent of the members of Consumers Union who owned belts actually used them, a much higher percentage than the national surveys would have suggested. And each new article about safety in *Consumer Reports* stimulated a greater number of inquiries from its readers about safety (see Appendix, Figure 1).[62]

State governments began to investigate the possibility of regulating vehicle design. The New York State Legislature's Committee on the Motor Vehicle, under the leadership of Edward Speno, visited Detroit in February 1961 to ask manufacturers to place anchorages and belts into all cars. Informed by Speno that New York would pass legislation requiring anchorages regardless of cooperation from producers, the industry (after many earlier refusals) finally agreed to drill secure holes in the chassis of automobiles so that seat belts would be easier for consumers to install.[63]

Fueled by the interest in safety, political activity at both state and federal levels increased. Late in 1961, Wisconsin enacted legislation requiring the installation of seat belts in the front seats of every new car sold after 1962. Within two years, twenty-three states had followed suit. In 1963, the United States Congress enacted legislation which, as of 1965, required seat belts in the front seats of all cars sold to the federal government. After hearings at which representatives of the Public Health Service, the National Safety Council, and other groups testified, Congress adopted legislation directing the General Services Administration to issue a list of safety features and other design characteristics to be required of all cars bought by the government.[64]

As public criticism of the automobile industry grew, the tone of the magazine became markedly militant. WE REGRET TO ANNOUNCE THE DEATH OF TWO HUNDRED AND FIFTEEN, OR PERHAPS TWO HUNDRED AND FIFTY, OF THE PEOPLE WHO READ THIS ARTICLE/THEY WILL BE KILLED IN A CAR CRASH WITHIN THE NEXT TWELVE MONTHS, a *Consumer Reports* headline declared, paraphrasing a British magazine. At one time determined to avoid the discussion of scientific problems in a moral context, the editors no longer found it possible, "either morally or in the simple context of objective reporting," to report on automobiles "without steady reference to their death-dealing and maiming characteristics." To illustrate its point, Consumers Union reviewed the statistics about highway deaths and listed the many hazards to be found in particular 1965 models including the Corvair, the Ford Custom, and others. *Consumer Reports* printed a scathing analysis of the prospects for safer cars by David Klein, a critic of the industry, and William Haddon, an outstanding proponent of accident research.[65]

Public pressure and government attention reached a dramatic peak early in 1966. Ralph Nader, interested in the problem of auto safety at least since 1956, in November 1965 published *Unsafe at Any Speed: The Designed-in Dangers of the American Automobile*. That book became a best seller in March 1966, when, at hearings held by Abraham Ribicoff of the Senate Subcommittee on Executive Reorganization, Nader confronted the president of General Motors with details about the defects of the Corvair and about the author's harassment by private detectives. The Ribicoff hearings transformed Nader into the most effective and well-known critic of the auto industry.[66]

Nader had offered Colston Warne a draft of his book in 1965, but Consumers Union delayed and then missed its chance to publish it because Crooks and others on the staff questioned its objectivity and doubted the reliability of some of the studies that Nader cited. CU, however, came quickly to acknowledge Nader's new centrality in the debate about auto safety. It alluded favorably to *Unsafe at Any Speed*, praised Nader, and in February and April of 1966 published pieces Nader had written. Nader would join the board of directors of Consumers Union in the following year.[67]

In April 1966, Consumers Union finally told its members that the cause of safer cars was moving forward. The automobile industry had begun to demonstrate "a conscience that is as healthy as its profits."

Gallup polls suggested that the public had come to consider automotive safety as an important national problem. Congressional committees were exploring proposals to promote better automotive design, including a national clearinghouse and standards-setting body, a prototype safety car project, and the compulsory application of GSA safety standards to all cars on the U.S. market. On September 6, 1966, President Johnson signed the National Traffic and Motor Vehicle Act and the Highway Safety Act. That legislation placed automobiles under the regulation of a National Highway Safety and Traffic Administration and created a special National Highway Safety Bureau to investigate problems that included vehicle design.[68]

Lawrence Crooks retired as the head of the Auto Division in August 1966, just as the first comprehensive package of federal safety legislation neared adoption. For thirty years, his reports had provided readers with material for the analysis of auto transportation. Hundreds of models were tested. Many guest columnists offered proposals for improved cars. In the years that followed 1966, when the problems of pollution from auto exhausts and the high cost of fuel joined safety as matters of social concern, the new heads of the Auto Division would try to incorporate the appropriate criteria into their work.[69]

There were times when CU's automotive coverage assumed a moralistic rather than a scientific tone. Late in the 1930s, CU had provided members with a political and social analysis of automobiles and of transportation, broadly considered, in *Millions on Wheels*. And in the mid-1960s, *Consumer Reports* suggested that ensuring highway safety amounted to a moral challenge to the national will. With these important exceptions, Consumers Union limited its role chiefly to test reports. If these reports did not solve problems, at least they exposed them. The test reports presented preferable alternatives to unsafe or unworthy products. They helped to create a demand for safety in the marketplace, and a more safety-conscious political climate.[70]

Consumers Union did not produce—nor did it intend to produce—a sustained, general perspective about the problem of travel in America, about the nature of the "car culture," or about the proper role of the federal government in finding or dictating solutions to transportation problems. Spurred by Ralph Nader, CU did use its budget surpluses to fund many innovative projects related to cars, notably the Center for Auto Safety, founded in 1970.[70] Consumers Union also published a CU edition of *The Great American Motion Sickness* (1971), concerned with problems of transportation. These grants and editions allowed CU to promote activism and to encourage discussions that it did not want to take upon itself directly. CU's commitment to testing had led it to leave theoretical social analysis and sustained political advocacy to groups less attached to objective study. Traditional safety proponents, Ralph Nader and his allies, and consumer-oriented politicians would adapt CU's technological criticism to their own needs.[71]

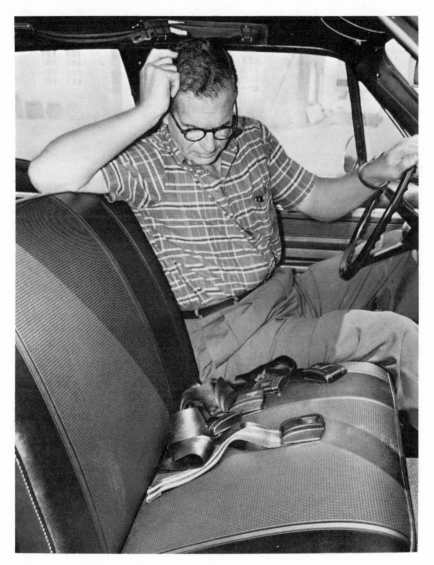

4.5 "What's Wrong with Seat Belts?," October 1968. Courtesy of Consumers Union.

CHAPTER V

Fallout in Food:
Exposing
Environmental
Contamination

In 1959, *Consumer Reports* warned its readers that because of atomic tests in the atmosphere, the milk that consumers drank contained radioactive strontium 90 (Sr-90). Before then, definite information about the danger of fallout from tests was not widely available. Popular writers discussed radiation, but not as an imminent hazard. Press coverage suggested that radioactive fallout might carry sickness or death to millions in the event of a nuclear war and that precautions needed to be taken around a nuclear test site; but there was little indication that test fallout posed a nationwide or worldwide threat to health. Consumers Union confirmed the possibility of such a threat from low levels of radiation and fostered a new debate about the nuclear arms race.[1]

Even in 1954, when the testing of an American H-bomb accidentally showered fallout on Japanese fishermen who then became seriously ill, the American public reacted with little collective sense of worry. As late as autumn 1955, fewer than 17 percent of a national sample could identify even the meaning of the word *fallout*. To the extent that fallout posed an immediate problem, it appeared to be a moral one: did the American government have a right to disturb the lives of natives in Pacific testing zones or in the American West to test weapons that seemed necessary to guard against a communist menace? Politicians and journalists argued that it did.[2]

During the first term of the Eisenhower administration, Secretary of State John Foster Dulles and others around him frightened the world with the prospect of total annihilation in a nuclear Armageddon. The Administration asserted that the likelihood of a war was reduced by a program of weapons development that assured the United States of nuclear superiority. "Self-imposed military inferiority," Dulles said, was "an invitation rather than a deterrent to war." By comparison with the prospect of a war caused by the failure to compete in the contest of military technology, the unverified risk from radioactive particles floating near a test site aroused very little concern. The apparent need for a nuclear bulwark against communist aggression eclipsed fears about the residue of atomic tests.[3]

The Growth of Scientific and Humanitarian Concern

Without access to appropriate scientific information, the critics of testing could not demonstrate the existence of fallout as a problem. The Atomic Energy Commission (AEC) and the Department of Defense (DOD) kept secret their internal debates about the dangers of H-bomb tests. Fallout, like other aspects of the weapons program, was supposedly a technical matter best left to government researchers. Responsible for promoting the rapid development of nuclear technology, the AEC showed little interest in publicizing the hazards and risks that were attached to its own operations, or even those of the Soviet Union. It reacted to questions about the safety of areas near test sites by releasing studies that argued that the H-bomb did not contaminate the surrounding air "unacceptably." Indeed, government officials announced that the test program would lead soon to a "humanitarian," "clean" H-bomb—with only short-lived and locally damaging radiation. The moral and scientific implausibility of a "humanitarian" weapon provoked skepticism among concerned observers.[4]

During 1955 *Science, Science Digest,* and the *Bulletin of Atomic Scientists,* anxious in any case about official secrecy, tried to find out more about fallout. Issues of *Science Newsletter* and the *Bulletin of Atomic Scientists* carried debates about whether tests should be suspended until more could be determined concerning the effects of radiation. Toward the middle of that year, *Christian Century, New Republic, Nation, Reporter,* and *Saturday Review* also called for more information. "Are Atomic Tests Dangerous?" Eric Sevareid wanted to know. The *New Yorker* amplified *Science Newsletter*'s report that the whole globe had been showered with radioactivity during a recent barrage of atomic tests.[5]

Prompted by an increasing anxiety about the effects of nuclear weapons projects, Adlai Stevenson called for a halt to tests as part of his

1956 election campaign. The nuclear arms race, he said, "threatens mankind with stark, merciless, bleak catastrophe." He called radioactive fallout, especially Sr-90, "the most dreadful poison in the world." Stevenson's remarks helped to spread an awareness of the radiation problem. A Gallup poll of May 1957 indicated that 52 percent of the public could provide a reasonable definition of fallout, while 31 percent of the sample registered concern about the safety of continued tests.[6]

The protests that followed linked citizens who feared the imminence of nuclear war with those who worried about the effects of fallout. In April 1957, Albert Schweitzer appealed to fifty nations to stop nuclear testing. Linus Pauling released a petition signed by 3,000 American and 8,000 foreign scientists, which called an international agreement to control fallout "imperative." Pauling indicated that his own position grew from "humanitarian, rather than scientific concerns." SANE, the National Committee for a Sane Nuclear Policy, began to organize around "the moral issue of stopping nuclear bomb tests." In a full-page advertisement in the *New York Times* that year, SANE maintained that the human community had a natural right "to live and grow, to breathe unpoisonous air, to work on uncontaminated soil." A group called "The Committee for 10,000 Babies" developed in California. Quakers and nonsectarian pacifist groups circulated antitesting petitions. As an international conference of scientists met in July at Pugwash, Nova Scotia, to discuss the worldwide implications of the testing of nuclear weapons, Norman Cousins declared that "the great debate" about fallout and nuclear tests had opened in earnest. By the year's end, the test-ban movement had gained considerable support on both moral and scientific grounds.[7]

In March 1958, the Soviet Union announced a unilateral suspension of its nuclear tests. Many Americans accepted the Soviet statement as an invitation to a universal halt. Responding to the Soviet initiative, the United States in August agreed to a moratorium. Throughout the world, scientists and public leaders expressed relief.[8]

The Consumer Interest in Fallout

The coverage that the media gave to the test-ban question expanded. Research about the effects of radiation, however, continued to be modest, especially when compared to the time and money devoted to nuclear development. Early in 1958, as attention to the problem of fallout grew, a scientist and an editor at CU became convinced that radioactive environmental contamination was potentially a consumer issue. They decided that a typical product-testing approach to the fallout problem might be useful.[9]

END BOMB TESTING

AND MOVE TOWARD PEACE

WHY

have 9,000 scientists, The World Council of Churches, Albert Schweitzer, Pope Pius XII, Gen. Omar Bradley, Eleanor Roosevelt and many others asked for an end to H-bomb tests and nuclear warfare?

HEAR

humanity's greatest problem discussed by—

Fri., April 18 — 8:15 p.m.

COOPER UNION — GREAT HALL
3rd Ave. and E. 8th St., Manhattan

ADMISSION FREE

REV. JOHN C. BENNETT
Dean of Faculty, Union Theological Seminary

COUNCILMAN STANLEY ISAACS
New York City Council

REPRESENTATIVE CHARLES O. PORTER
U. S. Representative, Washington

NORMAN THOMAS
Chairman, Post War Peace Council
American Elder Statesman
Author and Lecturer

DR. HUGH C. WOLFE
Chairman, American Federation of Scientists;
Professor of Physics, Cooper Union

The Deadly Nuclear Arms Race Can Be Stopped If You Also . . .

APPEAL for NUCLEAR SANITY

April 11th - 19th, 1958

SPONSORS

Adele Addison*
Michael Aronu**
Rev. Kenneth R. Baldwin
Rev. Donald C. Bell
Rev. Lloyd A. Berg
Dr. Algernon D. Black*
Dr. Alan R. Bleich*
Dr. LeRoy Bowman
Dr. Edmund M. Braun
Dr. Bess Cameron**
Sanford Clarke
Dr. Charles W. Collins
Norman Cousins*
Nathaniel Cullinan**
Dr. Dwight Durling
Rev. Phillips Elliot*
Father George B. Ford
Eleanor Clark French*
Dr. Erich Fromm*

Rabbi Israel Goldstein
Robert Gilmore**
Phillis Grunauer**
Florence D. Hamilton**
Rev. Donald Harrington*
Rabbi Isidor B. Hoffman*
Dr. John Haynes Holmes*
William R. Huntington*
Rev. James M. Hutchinson
Matthew Huxley
Stanley M. Isaacs*
Morris Isahewitz*
Annette Jameson**
Rev. William G. Kalaidjian
Donald Kaye*
Rabbi Edward E. Klein*
Rev. John M. Krumm*
Helen Lange**
Rev. John Howland Lathrop*

Dr. Walter J. Lear**
Dr. Harold Lenz
Rabbi Herschel Levin
David Livingston*
Anthony Mazzocchi**
Rev. Robert J. McCracken*
Rev. Donald W. McKinney
Yvonne McKinney**
Edward W. McVitty**
Carey McWilliams
Stewart Meacham*
Rabbi Max Mayer
Benjamin Miller**
Rev. Howard R. Moody
Lewis Mumford*
Rev. C. Kilmer Myers
Rev. A. J. Muste*
Tracy D. Mygatt*
Dr. Otto Nathan

Eva Newmark**
Rev. Alfred H. Rapp
Rev. Hartley C. Ray
Delbert B. Replogle
Rev. Paul W. Rishell**
Harry Rogers
Richard Schackman
Elmer L. Severinghaus
Rabbi Charles E. Shulman
Rabbi Howard Singer
Randolph B. Smith
Dr. Matthew Spetter*
Dr. Samuel Standard*
Dr. Arthur L. Swift, Jr.*

Dorothy Stout*
Irvin Seall
Norman Studer
Allen Taylor**
Norman Thomas*
James Warburg*
Dr. Carleton W. Washburne*
Rowland Watts*
Kenneth N. Whitlock
Dr. H. H. Wilson*
Dr. Hugh C. Wolfe**
Harold Wurf**

List incomplete

* Sponsor — New York Committee
** Executive Committee

Information about other meetings in the New York area
and about other activities which are part of this APPEAL may be obtained from:

THE GREATER NEW YORK COMMITTEE FOR SANE NUCLEAR POLICY
237 THIRD AVENUE, NEW YORK 3, N. Y. (GR 3-5998)

5.1 A handbill advertising a discussion of the humanitarian and religious issues related to the testing of atomic bombs and the arms race, 1958. Reproduced courtesy of New York Council of Citizens for a SANE World.

Dexter Masters, the executive director at Consumers Union, and Irving Michelson, then the head of the Special Projects Division, had been interested in atomic research for many years. Masters edited communications among atomic scientists on the Manhattan Project. Michelson, deeply affected by the destruction of Hiroshima, had turned down a job offer from Consumers Union in 1947 in order to stay in a student play about the Bomb which had a gloomy, doomsday ending. By 1958, both men held positions of authority at CU. They persuaded the board of directors and planning committees that fallout from the recent testing of nuclear weapons involved questions not only of foreign policy, but of the adulteration of food—a traditional consumer interest. Michelson took charge of planning an approach to the problem that would be suitable for the magazine.[10]

To begin with, Consumers Union corresponded with officials at the Atomic Energy Commission and the Public Health Service (PHS). CU also communicated with university scientists, among them Barry Commoner in Saint Louis, who had been working on the problems of radioactive contamination of the environment. Michelson discussed the intention of his organization with researchers at the Public Health Service, the Atomic Energy Commission, and at the Department of Agriculture (USDA).[11]

Michelson knew that Sr-90 could lodge in milk and thus be ingested by consumers; it surprised him, therefore, to learn that the surveillance of fallout in milk by the Public Health Service and the Atomic Energy Commission was perfunctory. Those agencies sampled milk for radioactivity only once a month in nine cities. They spot-checked milk in a few other locations, but the overall record was incomplete. The chief of the milk and food program of the health service and other government officials acknowledged these deficiencies and advised that CU could be of service if it verified those government figures that had been released about the contamination of milk. Michelson proposed to CU's technical director that "CU undertake to do a survey of strontium-90 in milk in fifty widely scattered areas in one month and that some of these areas be selected with a view to checking the PHS and AEC figures." He asked CU to find an unassailable authority to help plan and interpret the experiment and its results.[12]

The project was approved. During July and August of 1958, shoppers for CU, who ordinarily spent their time buying different household goods and appliances, bought quart samples of milk from different dairies throughout the country. The samples then were combined into *aliquots*, or fractional parts, for analysis. Personnel at Isotopes, Incorporated, a respected radiological laboratory in western New Jersey, helped the technicians and scientists at Consumer Union to develop appropriate ways to analyze, interpret, and present their measurements.[13]

CU counted on the tests to produce new information on a national scale. Scientists considered milk the primary route through which Sr-90 found its way into the bones of Americans, particularly into the bones of children whose growing skeletons absorbed the isotope more readily than did adult bones. A broad, snapshot view of the levels of contamination would give the permanent monitoring agencies—particularly the PHS—knowledge about the geographical variation of fallout levels and point to areas that needed additional study. Quickly and economically, CU could obtain an indication of the possible radioactive threat to coming generations.[14]

Sensible from a scientific standpoint, the decision to test milk also was a logical way to intensify popular interest in fallout. The dairy industry proudly declared that milk appeared on 95 percent of America's kitchen tables every day. According to public relations officials, milk enjoyed an enviable reputation as the country's most wholesome and nutritious beverage. To cast doubt on the wholesomeness of milk because of its radioactivity would be to suggest that Americans were losing their essential vitality because of atomic weaponry.[15]

By January 1959, the staff at CU had reviewed the results of the tests and sent review copies of an essay on strontium 90 to selected authorities for criticism. Despite differences of opinion, comment was favorable. Some officials at the AEC disagreed with CU's view that the meaning of radiation danger levels was not a clear one, but many of those inside the Public Health Service praised the essay. After clarifying the prose and modifying several details—but leaving the basic conclusions intact—CU sent the article to press as part of the March issue of *Consumer Reports*.[16]

"The Milk We Drink" appeared in March 1959, with restrained headlines and a subdued tone. With the help of a physicist at Cornell University, Consumers Union presented graphs, maps, and tables to illustrate the history and current status of radiation studies and to explain the tests of milk. CU found that the amount of Sr-90 in each gram of calcium in milk varied considerably throughout the country. Although all fifty of the readings—undertaken in forty-eight American and two Canadian cities—were below the limit set by the National Committee for Radiation Protection, this limit itself, CU wrote, was ambiguous. Significantly, the amount of Sr-90 in milk was rising, and the higher it rose, the greater were the risks of leukemia, cancer, and genetic mutation in present and future generations.[17]

Consumers Union based its conclusions on the knowledge that scientists remained uncertain about radiants. The individual consumer could do little to protect himself:

> This report cannot be ended with a clear recommendation. None exists. No doubt the Best Buy is milk without Sr-90, air without fallout, and adequate medical care without diagnostic X-rays. But none of these solutions are to be had, and it would be as foolish to stop drinking milk as it would be to refuse an X-ray for a broken limb. The surveys of the Sr-90 content of milk made by CU and by other agencies have demonstrated that there *is* a potential hazard. A judgment as to whether we are now within or without prudent limits depends on a variety of uncertain factors—ranging in character from the nature of bone growth to the problem of leukemia induction by X-rays—the answers to which have not yet been set by science.

According to *Consumer Reports,* the situation required immediate government action. This action would include an increased investigation of radiation problems with a wider, more frequent monitoring effort, and more intensive research about how concentrations of Sr-90 could be removed from soil and milk. The Public Health Service, CU concluded, rather than the Atomic Energy Commission, should supervise these expanded federal activities.

> Though the interest of the PHS in the matter has led it to equip and staff some very competent laboratories, it is still true that the overall problem has remained the province of the AEC. But it is hard to see why judgments on matters of public health should have to depend primarily on the reports of the very agency charged with the responsibility of manufacturing nuclear weapons, rather than on those of an agency whose specific job it is to safeguard the public's health. Without reflecting in any way on the AEC's competence or integrity, CU would support measures which would lead to thorough and independent investigations (as well as routine surveillance) by the Public Health Service on fundamental biological and control problems, wherever there is concern with fallout.

Consumer Reports also condemned nuclear testing. "It is the diplomat who holds the key to the solution of the base problem: cessation of nuclear explosions in the atmosphere." The end of tests, while stopping the production of fallout in peacetime, would also constitute a step toward arms limitation.[18]

The Consequences of Testing Milk

The immediate response to "The Milk We Drink" astounded its authors. Parents confused about fallout wrote to *Consumer Reports*. Within a week or two of publication, daily newspapers in the cities where milk had been tested printed digests of the magazine's findings.[19]

With varying degrees of accuracy, journalists cast headlines and wrote feature articles about the tests. The *New York Post*, anticipating the *CR* article on February 20, noted that Consumers Union predicted steadily rising, "potentially deadly levels of Sr-90." The Greater St. Louis Committee for Nuclear Information, a group formed a year earlier by scientists Barry Commoner, John Fowler, and concerned citizens in the community, helped the *Post-Dispatch* to print long and accurate discussions of fallout. On March 7, the *Washington Post* reported that CU was the first organization to publish fallout levels for milk in the District of Columbia. "Despite the steady rise in the radioactivity in foodstuffs," the newspaper editorialized, "no one seems to be keeping tabs on the amount of Sr-90 that's finding its way into the total diet these days." After an industrious Quebec reporter interviewed everyone from the city's helpless director of public health to unprepared dairy officials throughout the city, the *Quebec Chronicle-Telegraph* published a front-page banner: "TESTS SHOW MILK CONTAMINATED, HEALTH DIRECTOR SHOWS SURPRISE. . . ." The report of the *Norfolk Ledger-Dispatch* included a picture of a housewife's hand reaching for a bottle of milk and the ominous statement that Norfolk was "high among cities in Strontium content." Medical journals and union newsletters wrote about the study. *Dog World* magazine alerted its readers to the possible contamination of what it called "the favorite canine food," milk.[20]

The milk industry considered the Consumers Union article and its aftermath to be a disaster. One month *before* the article by Consumers Union appeared, the back cover of *Consumer Reports* had rattled members of the Milk Industry Foundation. The magazine then had announced that next month's issue would discuss strontium 90 in milk. Beside a picture of a child with a glass of milk in her hand, the testing organization announced the completion of tests "designed to provide an authoritative assessment of this fallout hazard in the milk that many millions of us drink." Ernest B. Kellogg, executive secretary of the Milk Foundation, a lobby and publicity group for major milk distributors, complained that the back cover was unnecessarily sensational. Images of radioactive milk might occur subliminally in the minds of everyone who saw it. The dairy industry anticipated widespread concern about radioactivity in milk products. Retail consumption of whole milk already suffered from demographic changes, worries about cholesterol, and rising sales of soda pop. Dairymen hoped to avoid adding radiation to their list of woes.[21]

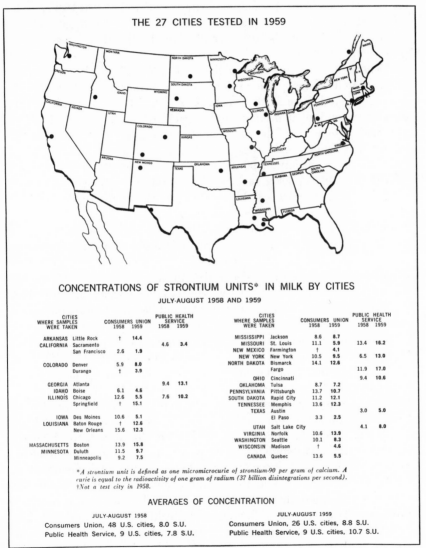

THE 27 CITIES TESTED IN 1959

CONCENTRATIONS OF STRONTIUM UNITS* IN MILK BY CITIES
JULY-AUGUST 1958 AND 1959

CITIES WHERE SAMPLES WERE TAKEN		CONSUMERS UNION 1958	1959	PUBLIC HEALTH SERVICE 1958	1959	CITIES WHERE SAMPLES WERE TAKEN		CONSUMERS UNION 1958	1959	PUBLIC HEALTH SERVICE 1958	1959
ARKANSAS	Little Rock	†	14.4			MISSISSIPPI	Jackson	8.6	8.7		
CALIFORNIA	Sacramento			4.6	3.4	MISSOURI	St. Louis	11.1	5.9	13.4	16.2
	San Francisco	2.6	1.9			NEW MEXICO	Farmington	†	4.1		
						NEW YORK	New York	10.5	9.5	6.5	13.0
COLORADO	Denver	5.9	8.0			NORTH DAKOTA	Bismarck	14.1	12.6		
	Durango	†	3.9				Fargo			11.9	17.0
						OHIO	Cincinnati			9.4	10.6
GEORGIA	Atlanta			9.4	13.1	OKLAHOMA	Tulsa	8.7	7.2		
IDAHO	Boise	6.1	4.6			PENNSYLVANIA	Pittsburgh	13.7	10.7		
ILLINOIS	Chicago	12.6	5.5	7.6	10.2	SOUTH DAKOTA	Rapid City	11.2	12.1		
	Springfield	†	15.1			TENNESSEE	Memphis	13.6	12.3		
						TEXAS	Austin			3.0	5.0
IOWA	Des Moines	10.6	5.1				El Paso	3.3	2.5		
LOUISIANA	Baton Rouge	†	12.6			UTAH	Salt Lake City			4.1	8.0
	New Orleans	15.6	12.3			VIRGINIA	Norfolk	10.6	13.9		
						WASHINGTON	Seattle	10.1	8.3		
MASSACHUSETTS	Boston	13.9	15.8			WISCONSIN	Madison	†	4.6		
MINNESOTA	Duluth	11.5	9.7								
	Minneapolis	9.2	7.5			CANADA	Quebec	13.6	5.5		

*A strontium unit is defined as one micromicrocurie of strontium-90 per gram of calcium. A curie is equal to the radioactivity of one gram of radium (37 billion disintegrations per second).
†Not a test city in 1958.

AVERAGES OF CONCENTRATION

JULY-AUGUST 1958	JULY-AUGUST 1959
Consumers Union, 48 U.S. cities, 8.0 S.U.	Consumers Union, 26 U.S. cities, 8.8 S.U.
Public Health Service, 9 U.S. cities, 7.8 S.U.	Public Health Service, 9 U.S. cities, 10.7 S.U.

5.2 The table that presented CU's measurements of Sr-90 in milk, February 1960. Note the few cities in which the Public Health Service had taken measurements. Courtesy of Consumers Union.

As dairymen feared, retail sales of fluid milk in March 1959 were lower than ordinary. Daily receipts of milk from producers fell below the level of either the preceding or following March by 2 to 3 percent nationally. Executive Secretary Kellogg of the Milk Foundation, in another letter to Consumers Union, blamed *Consumer Reports* for trying to increase its circulation at the dairy industry's expense. Morris Kaplan, CU's technical director, rightly replied that the article specifically advised against discontinuing the use of milk, but the foundation was not appeased.[22]

The industry assured the public that milk was safe, but it soon discovered, to its dismay, that a reference to radiation and milk at the same time connected them in the consumer's mind. Trade associations then decided to continue to promote milk on the basis of its nutritional value— without any mention of the problem of radioactivity. Dairy councils suggested that retailers advertise accordingly to counteract the damaging publicity about strontium 90 as much as possible. But producers and distributors alike quickly realized that publicity campaigns would not suffice. In order to restore public confidence, the dairy industry needed a clean bill of health from government agencies.[23]

Public confusion, inquiries from the mass media, and the appeals of industrial leaders for assistance all focused on the need for action by the government. City and state departments of health and state agricultural departments, although besieged with requests to monitor Sr-90 in milk, were not equipped to do so. Dairy industry technologists and agricultural inspectors regularly analyzed milk for fat and bacteria factors, but not for radioactivity. Only the federal government could act effectively.[24]

Federal agencies, committees, and commissions spoke more openly about their work soon after the Consumers Union report. Dr. Willard F. Libby of the AEC told the Joint Committee on Atomic Energy in late February that the commission was concerned about Sr-90 levels in wheat, but that it was certain the average consumption levels for Sr-90 were "well below the maximum possible level." The Public Health Service, the Food and Drug Administration, and even the Bureau of Fisheries testified that further study of fallout problems was crucial. Each agency maintained that it lacked the resources to pursue the subject comprehensively. On March 10, an advisory commission to the Public Health Service recommended that the PHS be granted control of surveillance programs. Two days later, Secretary of Health, Education and Welfare Arthur Flemming revealed that he would try to increase the funds available to study the safe limits of Sr-90 in food and water. Flemming announced that "all milk thus far sampled has been well within this limit," but the problem of radiation would "be with us from now on." Beyond a request for two million dollars for radiation studies by the National Insti-

How Milk Protects you from Fallout....

(Strontium-90 is the most dangerous radioactive contaminant that results from fallout -- because it is long-lasting and can attack the human bones.)

1. MILK CONTAINS LESS STRONTIUM-90 THAN OTHER FOODS

The current levels of strontium units in the plant portion of our diet probably averages 5 to 20 times as high as the levels in milk and may well be higher in other areas.

5 units in milk; 210 to 628 in cabbage; 37 to 50 in potatoes; 1,137 in peas; 34 to 200 in sweet corn; 110 in apples; 96 to 4,420 in lettuce; etc.

2. YOU ARE SAFEGUARDED THROUGH THE COW

Cows take into their systems only about 5 percent of the strontium-90 they consume when feeding upon these (contaminated) plants. And cows secrete in their milk only 1/5 of the strontium-90 they take into their systems each day . . . We are dealing here with minute quantities of radio active materials.

3. MILK AND DAIRY PRODUCTS REDUCE THE SR-90 IN YOUR BONES

The most significant aspect of the data released during the past years is that the high calcium level in milk is the agent in the diet which will help reduce the relative bone deposition of strontium-90 . . . The data suggest that increased milk consumption is a means of further lowering the level of strontium-90 deposited in our bones.

In the Event of an Atomic Holocaust

In the event of an atomic holocaust as a result of nuclear warfare, milk will still be the best food. There has been developed a standby process for removing strontium-90 from milk. The pilot plant at Beltsville, Md. can remove as much as 98 percent of strontium-90. Also, the addition to milk of an equal amount of calcium can be just as effective as removing 50 percent of the strontium-90.

No Foreseeable Danger from Fallout

Watching TV a couple of hours a day may give more radiation to a child than the milk he drinks where fallout is said to be showing up.

Although nuclear testing has been resumed, levels of atmospheric contamination are still well below the point of any serious concern and are expected to remain so for the foreseeable future . . .

The safety of our milk supply was not in jeopardy when the strontium-removing research program was initiated; it is not in jeopardy today.

5.3   The dairy industry responded to public concern about the wholesomeness of milk by distributing leaflets like the one above, which called milk the "best food for the atomic age." Reproduced courtesy of the National Milk Producers Federation.

tutes of Health, he asked for an increase of funds for surveillance to an amount of one and a half million dollars for the coming year.[25]

Shaken by public opinion, Congress became critical of the Atomic Energy Commission. On March 21 Senator Clinton Anderson of New

Mexico, chairman of the Joint Committee on Atomic Energy, forced the release of previously classified letters. These revealed that fallout was descending into the atmosphere at a rate much faster than the AEC had contended previously, and at a disproportional rate into latitude bands that included the United States. Libby announced that new hearings of the Joint Committee would consider those matters when the Subcommittee on Radiation reconvened in May.[26]

On March 23 Senators Anderson and Hubert Humphrey of Minnesota accused the AEC of withholding and "playing down" information about fallout. The chairman of the commission replied that a presidential advisory committee would meet to review the matter. President Eisenhower commented that to his knowledge there had been no suppression of information. Nonetheless, the Surgeon-General's National Advisory Commission on Radiation on the following day agreed with the recommendation of the PHS advisory committee and advocated prompt transferal of all radiation-control programs relating to health from the AEC to the PHS. The Advisory Commission noted a basic conflict between a concern for new uses of atomic energy and a concern for the public health, as well as heightened respect for the dangers of fallout: "There is no such thing as a safe level of radiation."[27]

Congressional action followed. Senator Lister Hill and Congressman Kenneth Roberts, both of Alabama, introduced legislation on April 10 to place every fallout and radiation-protection program under the control of the Public Health Service. Renewed fears of test resumption and the publication of a Lamont Laboratory study, which showed that the amount of Sr-90 in the bones of children had doubled during 1957, maintained the pressure for passage. In September Clinton Anderson's bill, amending the original AEC enabling legislation, became law. The Public Health Service, now equipped with much of the authority for surveillance that Consumers Union had recommended in "The Milk We Drink," expanded its research relating to fallout and announced a two and a half million dollar budget available for the purpose.[28]

Follow-Up

After the March report, Consumers Union continued the effort to find out more about radiation. Initially, CU had decided to promote the reform of the radiation-control programs by creating popular awareness of their inadequacies. By May 1959, the national sense of urgency about the unknown risks of fallout appeared to be dissipating because of the efforts of the government to rectify whatever apparent regulatory failings existed. Michelson, Masters, and the Consumers Union Board, however, were reluctant to stop radiation studies simply because the government momentarily was taking its monitoring task more seriously. It seemed important for an independent group like CU to keep an ongoing watch on the problem of fallout.[29]

During the spring of 1959, Consumers Union formulated a strategy for addressing the fallout problem in the future. The organization had learned the value of repeating tests of items like cigarettes or cars to check for progress made or remaining deficiencies. It decided to follow up the first set of tests for radioactivity in milk with another identical set. Consumers Union also lent its support to a relatively simple, attention-getting method that the St. Louis Nuclear Information Committee used to measure the Sr-90 absorbed by infants. The committee analyzed baby teeth collected from the offspring of parents in the community. Consumers Union paid for some initial laboratory analysis and helped to publicize the study.[30]

The new plans required more money than Consumers Union could afford. Eager to go on with the monitoring, the board departed from its policy not to accept outside support. While some in the organization expressed reservations, Consumers Union decided that receiving money from either the PHS or AEC would not bias research or create any conflict of interest. Michelson took charge of a new Department of Public Service Projects and looked for government grants in order to continue. By October 1959, the Public Service Department, with the help of grants from the AEC and PHS, had begun to examine not only Sr-90 in milk, but several radioisotopes in the total diet of typical Americans. Such a study, it was hoped, would bring the radioactive contamination of food into focus as a general problem, of which milk was only part.[31]

While the total diet studies proceeded, CU renewed its criticism of government monitoring policies. Michelson told the secretary of Health Education and Welfare in January of 1960 that milk sampling techniques of the government might "be adequate for research purposes . . . but not for the purpose of determining the Sr-90 content of milk which is reaching consumer markets." In February, CU's tests revealed a disturbing trend of increasing radiation levels, especially when compared with the conclusions drawn by the PHS and AEC sampling programs. In June, CU reported that products other than milk accounted for more human consumption of Sr-90 than scientists previously had believed. Consumers Union applauded the announcement that a new system would monitor over sixty milksheds across the nation; but it reminded the public that there were more than two hundred metropolitan areas in the country. The Food and Drug Administration, an agency with "a mountainous objective—a continuing study of radioactivity in food"—had labored "to bring forth a mouse."[32]

Another way to attract public interest was to explore the possibility of food decontamination and of protection against the effects of consuming radioactive milk. In the fall of 1960, the Public Service Department considered methods by which consumers could avoid the retention of strontium 90 and advised that calcium pills might help consumers to reduce their absorption of radioactive elements. In August 1961, CU repeated that advice and urged the government to press on with the development of a commercial process to purify contaminated milk. In a pioneering article that suggested the potential danger of storing the radioactive wastes generated by nuclear power plants, the magazine emphasized that

"THERE MUST BE SOME WAY THAT'S MORE SCIENTIFIC"

HERBLOCK IN THE WASHINGTON POST AND TIMES HERALD

5.4 "There Must Be Some Way That's More Scientific,"
1959 Herblock cartoon printed in the *Washington Post*.
Reprinted with permission of the Herblock Syndicate.
the Herblock Syndicate.

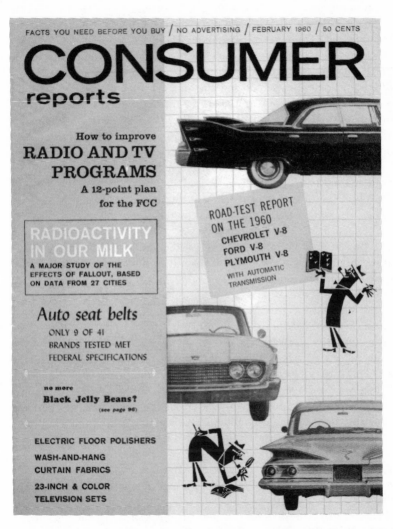

FACTS YOU NEED BEFORE YOU BUY / NO ADVERTISING / FEBRUARY 1960 / 50 CENTS

CONSUMER
reports

How to improve
RADIO AND TV
PROGRAMS
A 12-point plan
for the FCC

RADIOACTIVITY IN OUR MILK
A MAJOR STUDY OF THE
EFFECTS OF FALLOUT, BASED
ON DATA FROM 27 CITIES

Auto seat belts
ONLY 9 OF 41
BRANDS TESTED MET
FEDERAL SPECIFICATIONS

no more
Black Jelly Beans?
(see page 96)

ELECTRIC FLOOR POLISHERS

WASH-AND-HANG
CURTAIN FABRICS

23-INCH & COLOR
TELEVISION SETS

ROAD-TEST REPORT
ON THE 1960
CHEVROLET V-8
FORD V-8
PLYMOUTH V-8
WITH AUTOMATIC
TRANSMISSION

5.5   Cover, *Consumer Reports*, February 1960. Courtesy of Consumers Union.

in the face of these wastes, as well as the widening use of radiants in medicine and industry, and of the increasing threat of new atomic tests, no one knew for certain how dangerous accumulations of Sr-90 in the body would be in the years to come.[33]

During the Berlin crisis, also in August of 1961, the Soviet Union resumed nuclear testing. Fifteen days later the United States once more began testing, underground. The press, radio, and television were alert to the renewal of radioactive pollution. *Christian Century* wanted "the truth about fallout." *U.S. News* interviewed Linus Pauling about the effects of fallout. *Time* referred to fallout debris as "hot cargo."[34]

Consumers Union asked for action that would neutralize the effects of the resumption of testing. Its second report on the total diet studies, confined to data collected during the moratorium, recorded slight declines in levels of radiation. In January 1962, however, calculations by the Atomic Energy Commission predicted that because of the new Russian tests, Sr-90 in milk would soon more than double. Milk, warned CU, would be "loaded with Sr-90 to an extent which will require control measures." *Consumer Reports* called for pasture lands to be limed with uncontaminated calcium, and, "if possible, decontamination of the milk itself while it's undergoing processing at the dairies."[35]

The grim predictions and subsequent publicity disturbed the milk industry once again. This time, however, the dairy business was prepared. Magazines that reported the predictions of the AEC received counterarguments from dairy scientists and technologists. Dairy experts wrote to Consumers Union and protested that to call milk "loaded with Sr-90" smacked of sensationalism rather than truth. The consumption of milk had declined recently, and the executive director of one state dairy organization again blamed the downturn on articles like the one in the January *Consumer Reports*.[36]

The press releases of the dairy industry reminded people that the Public Health Service checked milk regularly, and declared it to be safe. Since a cow's digestive tract filtered out much of the Sr-90 in grain and vegetable products, industry spokesmen claimed that milk formed the best possible *defense* against radiation. Consumers Union never denied that milk constituted a relative benefit to the diet. CU correctly argued that the general level of consumption of Sr-90 was accelerating dangerously, that milk was one of the products through which Sr-90 passed to humans, and that the level of the contaminant needed to be stabilized or reduced.[37]

President Kennedy, like President Eisenhower, performed a notable service for the milk industry by assuring the nation that if milk were to be contaminated unacceptably, it would never reach the public. "The milk supply," he said, "offers no hazards from fallout. On the contrary, milk remains one of the best sources of nutrition for children and adults." The Research Council of the National Academy of Sciences released a statement in the spring of 1961 which said that the milk supply was perfectly safe. Hood Dairy, after meeting with its public relations and market research consultants, decided to spend $12,000 in November and December of that year on a radio, television, newspaper, and personal publicity campaign. The campaign was designed to provide "a public service which had the side result of helping improve Hood's image as a responsible citizen and a progressive firm."[38]

By the end of 1961, Americans appeared no longer to consider radiation in milk to be a serious difficulty. New government surveillance and research programs, combined with the public relations efforts of the dairy industry, promoted confidence in the product. Most important, the discovery that the predictions made by the AEC of high fallout from the latest tests were inaccurate allayed popular concern. A Gallup poll in late November 1961 showed that Americans again feared test fallout far less than the escalation of the cold war and the Soviet nuclear threat. Preoccupied with the Kennedy administration's new program of civil defense preparedness,* fears about low-level radiation diminished.[39]

The campaign to build fallout shelters hardly reassured Consumers Union about the adequacy of the monitoring network or the safety of the food supply. Quite the contrary, the testing of nuclear weapons continued, fallout increased, and CU continued to express worry about the safety of the food supply. But after several years of practice, the federal government, like the dairy industry, was better able to defend its monitoring programs. On June 5, 1962, Michelson once more told a Radiation Standards Subcommittee hearing that the monitoring networks remained inadequate and even misleading—particularly with reference to isotopes other than strontium 90. Michelson mentioned iodine 131, dangerous to the thyroid gland, as an example. This time, the Public Health Service crushed his argument by releasing a long-secret report which showed that the health service had been following levels of strontium and iodine carefully; presumably the PHS stood ready to take action if the levels became too high.[40]

Acting on the basis of information from its monitoring network, the Public Health Service did divert fluid milk from the retail market for the first time in July 1962. In Salt Lake City, levels of iodine 131 reached a concentration that the PHS considered dangerous. Milk was routed into

---

*In a report that was partly serious and partly tongue-in-cheek, CU contributed to the chilling philosophical debates about the desirability of surviving a nuclear holocaust and the ethical dilemmas presented by owning an individual fallout shelter by testing shelters to see whether survival even was possible. Just as the staff tested other products, it rated fallout shelters on the basis of cost, reliability and anticipated performance—under various kinds of nuclear attack. Consumers Union determined that it could not rate as "acceptable" any shelter that an individual consumer could afford to build.

storage or into processing as cheese while the iodine decayed. This re-kindled fear about fallout. In the *New York Times*, a full-page advertise-ment from SANE displayed a picture of a quarantined milk bottle with the caption "HAS IT COME TO THIS?" International scientists, contem-porary celebrities, clergymen, and members of the civil rights move-ment—about a hundred persons in all—seized the incident as compelling proof of the need for a nuclear test-ban treaty.[41]

At Moscow in August 1963, American, British, and Russian repre-sentatives agreed to a partial ban on aboveground testing. Shortly afterward, Consumers Union published what turned out to be its last article about radioactive contamination of the food supply, an "interim" report on the total diet studies. The Moscow Treaty, Consumers Union observed, may not have gone far toward easing the tensions of the cold war, but it did bring to a temporary halt the contamination that Russians and Americans cast recklessly into the world around them.[42]

The approach that Consumers Union took to the fallout problem revealed weaknesses and strengths that were characteristic of CU's con-sumer advocacy during the 1950s. Product testing by its nature was re-stricted to goods that consumers bought in the marketplace, yet it raised awareness about collective social issues that extended beyond traditional consumer interests. CU's political and social analysis stopped short of a head-on assault on the problem of environmental contamination, but other groups dedicated to ending the nuclear arms race used the informa-tion that CU supplied to suit their purposes.

Consumer Reports took on the issue of fallout in food only until 1963, but over the next two decades the magazine continued to consider the possibility of different radioactive hazards—from X rays, color televisions, microwave ovens, and other consumer goods. For more than twenty years, remarkably, CU did not report on the safety of nuclear power plants; but when an accident at the Three Mile Island nuclear plant in Pennsylvania in 1979 prompted another look at low-level radioactive hazards, a younger generation of activists raised many of the same con-cerns that Consumers Union raised earlier about weapons tests—questions about the safety of the food supply, the adequacy of monitoring, about possible conflicts between the regard of government for promoting nuclear development and its interest in protecting public health, and worries about the dangers of environmental contamination. To persuade the public of these dangers, the new generation of reformers would try to develop the kinds of reputable scientific evidence that Consumers Union knew how to provide, and had provided in the past.[43]

CHAPTER VI

Science and Reform

MOST CONSUMER GROUPS were organized to confront particular issues, and then disintegrated in several years or less. Consumers Union institutionalized its method, not its interest in any single issue. This, more than anything else, explains its success. In 1961, Colston Warne attributed the vitality of Consumers Union to "the championship of an idea whose time was ripe." "An increasingly well-educated America, fortified by scientific techniques, was inevitably bound to develop an agency responsible to consumers," he suggested. In three decades of struggle Consumers Union established itself among the most effective and durable organizations that wed the power and persuasive appeal of positivist science to reform journalism.[1]

To explore fundamental reasons for the popular appeal of positivist science would require a different study. Such a study would include, at the least, an extended analysis of the history of the middle-class standard of utility in America, of the idea of progress, and of historical developments in such fields as medicine, law, economics, and sociology. "America is a civilization founded on science and rooted in its achievements," Max Lerner wrote in 1957. "The congruity between American science and the driving spirit of American political and economic development was the congruity of élan and energy." The enlistment of scientific authority to rationalize political and economic objectives represents a recurrent theme in American history.[2]

By the late 1920s, when independent product testing started, many research organizations had come into being, chiefly to provide empirical support and to solve problems for businesses and governments. Profit-making market research firms developed psychological and statistical techniques to provide "scientific" explanations of purchasing behavior. Nonprofit research institutes, including the Carnegie Institute (1902), the Carnegie Endowment for International Peace (1910), the Mellon Institute

(1913), the Batelle Institute (1923), the Kettering Foundation (1927), and many others were chartered, as was the Brookings Institution (1927), "to promote . . . scientific research, training and publication in the broad fields of economics, government administration and the political and social sciences generally, involving the study . . . of economic, social and political facts and principles." The labor movement, the Communist party and the Catholic church established research institutes that utilized the sciences or social sciences.[3]

Consumers Union provided the consumer movement with its own objective base. The particular technique of scientific testing that Consumers Union adopted splendidly suited the purpose of reaching the widest possible American audience, especially in the period between the beginning of World War II and the late 1960s; Consumers Union tested the world of merchandising at the same time that formal examinations emerged as common instruments for evaluating most aspects of life. In schools, nationwide achievement and intelligence testing had been routine since the 1920s. On radio and television, quiz shows used tests as entertainment. "By the second world war," Jacques Barzun has written, "testing by check-mark was established practice everywhere in American life—in the school system, in business, in the professions, in the administration of law and in the work of hospitals and institutions for the mentally handicapped. The production and administration of tests was an industry employing many hard-working and dedicated people."[4]

The tests that Consumers Union used as the backbone of its presentations impressed readers with their depth and apparent objectivity. The language of the fallout reports or the cigarette studies, for example, was chosen to sound authoritative and neutral. *Consumer Reports* reminded its readers of the impartiality of its researchers and its meticulous process of checking and double-checking each report. The scholarly apparatus of footnotes was missing, but all of CU's arguments were expressed in an objective, unambiguous, confident, scientific style that made accessible the findings of CU's researchers and eliminated pretentious or exaggerated jargon. The style was closer to that of *Scientific American* than to journals like the *Nation,* the *New Republic,* or *Harper's.* Consumers Union preferred publishing technically informed findings to unsubstantiated moral or political convictions. A scientific rather than a moralistic editorial posture would best move readers and earn their respect.

From the beginning, the methods of empirical science lent respectability and legitimacy to an otherwise suspect radicalism. Like the militant industrial labor movement of the 1930s, the radical consumer movement of that decade had provoked fear and suspicion. Two years before the formation of Consumers Union, in 1934, Warne had written in the *Annals of the American Academy* that "nothing short of a revolution will substantially alter the character of the business system, or its ally, advertising." Malinda Orlin, a political scientist, has written that as far as the American public of the 1930s was concerned, "the consumer leaders were radicals who insisted that consumer protection demanded reorganization of the basic economic and political structures. . . ." This was especially true after the violent split between Consumers' Research and Consumers Union and after the bitter accusations of J. B. Matthews.[5]

When the bounds of permissible dissent narrowed after the war, and when the anticommunist hysteria widened during the 1950s, the testing method shielded CU from severe criticism. There had been no articles in *Consumer Reports* about consumers as a class, and few essays directly concerned with corporate rule or capitalist hegemony. Discussions of the relation between the labor movement and the consumer movement virtually disappeared after 1948. *Consumer Reports* had become a magazine of technological and social criticism, not a radical journal of political economy.[6]

In choosing the path they did, those who guided CU agreed to take part in expensive technological explorations. These required millions of dollars per year to execute properly. The businesses and agencies whose products Consumers Union evaluated usually enjoyed far superior resources, which they used to respond to criticism. Ford, Chrysler, and General Motors each spent more money designing a single model of car than Consumers Union spent on its entire testing budget; the tobacco and dairy industry associations spent larger sums advertising their products than Consumers Union could spend on its entire operation. Despite CU's relatively meager resources, it managed to accomplish much because it could decide selectively which aspects of a finished product it wanted to test, and when it would conduct a test. As a high court of technological utility, Consumers Union usually could choose the time and circumstance of its review.

The reality of limited resources, however, restricted the expansion of the organization. The purchase of equipment needed to test cigarettes could not be justified by the limited use that Consumers Union would make of it. CU learned, when involved in the fallout studies, for example, that to become involved in basic rather than applied scientific research required more money than it could afford. A regular program of crash testing cars was beyond the means of the organization. Many tests required specialized skills that were unavailable to CU at the wages it paid.

A lack of funds also kept Consumers Union from considering the problem of distribution with the same intensity that it directed at production. Consumers Union could investigate manufactured goods with relative ease, but the limited size of its staff and budget made rating thousands of retail and wholesale outlets extremely difficult. Similarly, the services of doctors, dentists, lawyers, and others were hard to rate; they could be discussed only in general terms. Some of the most important aspects of consumer problems—aspects that would have made Consumers Union's criticism more complete—were not analyzed effectively.

Beyond the constraints imposed by financial considerations, the method itself imposed limitations on the scope of reform. Product testing was reactive rather than preventative in nature: as a private organization without the power of government, Consumers Union tested items after they became available to the public, not before. This meant, in practice, that CU could have at best a palliative effect on the abuses of the marketplace. CU might improve the quality of goods in an evolutionary fashion, but it could not have the immediate, massive impact on the contours of the consumer culture that Robert Lynd, David Riesman, and others hoped for.[7]

The imperatives of the method, furthermore, restricted the issues that Consumers Union explored and the way these issues were developed. The directors of Consumers Union were pragmatically oriented: they probed questions that their technique would be likely to illuminate, or else they looked for some facet to an important issue for which testing would be appropriate. Feature articles or columns addressed to general social problems had impact, but the stature of the organization rested upon its ability to sift scientific literature and to conduct its own tests.

Although Colston Warne, Dexter Masters, Mildred Brady, Edward Brecher, Irving Michelson, and many others connected with the organization resisted the suggestion that any important social problem could be addressed strictly through quantitative means or that philosophical questions had technological answers, the format and thrust of the magazine implied as much—that a world of nuclear weapons might be made safe through the decontamination of fallout; that seat belts or emission controls would produce safe transportation; that the quality of life itself would be better if the quality of goods improved. Intended or not, these conclusions were reached by segments of the readership of *Consumer Reports*.[8]

The logical error that provided moral problems with technical solutions may have been encouraged by the method, but it was not intrinsic to it. John Dewey, a supporter of consumer testing and one Warne knew personally, explained in *The Quest for Certainty* (1929) that good scientists understood that the knowledge they provided was primarily aimed not at inner truths but at an immediate level of behavioral reality:

> The search for "efficient causes" instead of for final causes, for extrinsic relations instead of intrinsic forms, constitutes the aim

of science. . . . It signifies a search for those relations on which the occurrence of real qualities and values depends, by means of which we can regulate their occurrence.

In spite of warnings that technological defects were symptomatic of deeper problems ("It is the diplomat who holds the key to the solution of the base problem"), many readers assumed that technological solutions were the most important solutions, or the only ones possible.[9]

Placing exclusive trust in scientific studies meant discounting both subjective evidence and the subjective research of "committed" reformers. Emphasizing its objectivity, Consumers Union placed distance between itself and groups less attached to objective methods. In the smoking controversy, this meant working largely apart from traditional antismoking groups and within the world of medical and epidemiological research. In the case of auto safety it led the Automotive Division to disparage—at first—the fairness of Ralph Nader's *Unsafe at Any Speed*. In the case of fallout, it meant focusing on a scientific question—the adequacy of the network for monitoring radiation—rather than on moral and political objections to testing weapons that SANE and other groups focused on. This meant eschewing the "subjective" analysis of marxist, socialist, progressive, or politically conservative groups. It meant being cautious about offering policy prescriptions.

For the employees of Consumers Union, the cost of scientific conservatism was a degree of isolation from others who worked toward similar objectives through different methods. As an institution, however, CU generally profited from the distance that it established between itself and less objective organizations. Radical consumer groups argued during the later 1960s and 1970s that Consumers Union underutilized its power and influence and alienated potential allies when it moved cautiously. "A sleeping giant," Ralph Nader called CU. Consumers Union reacted by noting its enhanced reputation in several scientific circles, its growing grant program to sustain radical consumer advocacy, its influence when it chose to take a strong position, and its rising circulation.[10]

As critics suggested, the insistence on responsible objectivity may have been more than a commitment to a successful strategy of impartiality. It may have been a substitute for the willingness of Consumers Union to take bold positions. Alvin Gouldner, a scholar concerned with the history of positivist sociology, wrote that objectivity is "the way one comes to terms and makes peace with a world one does not like but will not oppose."

Objectivity transforms the nowhere of exile into a positive and valued social location . . . it transforms the weakness of internal "refuge" into the superiority of principled aloofness. Objectivity is the ideology of those who are alienated and politically homeless.

Did Consumers Union take refuge from ideology through the use of its objective method? To the extent that it refused to support positions that its testing program or other research could not sanction, the organization considered itself to be correct and responsible. Formally, Consumers Union acknowledged that complete objectivity was not possible. "Ratings, even when based on laboratory tests, represent in large measure opinions and not simply a compilation of scientific data," CU pointed out in its very first issue and occasionally thereafter.[11]

Those who directed Consumers Union, furthermore, did not objectify the politics of the organization itself. The tests were objective, but the decisions about what items to test, which criteria to use, what questions to ask—these were value judgments made by the board, management, staff, and membership. How much money should be spent on a given test? How frequently should tests be repeated? Should special attention be given to products used by lower-income consumers? Should Consumers Union rate fallout shelters? Health care systems? These decisions were made in the context of a commitment to the themes of consumer protest and of disenchantment with the structure of the marketplace as it existed.

Consumers Union worked from the assumption that it was socially beneficial to expose the victimization of consumers and to heighten their collective identity. To critics, fostering the identity of people as consumers amounted to accepting a marketplace view of the world. "Once you describe yourself as a consumer you've become the problem," argued Nicholas Johnson, himself a consumer advocate. "The people recognize themselves in their commodities," wrote Herbert Marcuse. "They find their soul in their automobile, hi-fi set, split-level home, kitchen equipment. The very mechanism which ties the individual to his society has changed, and social control is anchored in the new needs which it has produced."[12]

Clearly Consumers Union could not have thrived as it did during the period studied here, in a culture that was less well integrated in economic terms or weaker in its faith in the virtues of abundance. A national publication such as *Consumer Reports* could not have existed without a national marketplace and without uniform attributes in the products it tested. Sales of the magazine, furthermore, seem to have been related directly to swings in the business cycle during the early 1970s. To contemporary critics these facts suggested that *Consumer Reports* provided a functional aid to the consumer culture, rather than fundamental criticism of it.[13]

The assertion that Consumers Union operated within a limited horizon due to its testing approach is strengthened by the centrality of appeals to self-interest that dominated each of the cases studied here. The reports on smoking, for example, considered the effects of cigarettes on those who purchased the packs and smoked them, but were scarcely concerned with nonsmokers (nonbuyers) in a smoking environment. The automotive coverage concentrated on the safety concerns of car buyers: that coverage paid more attention to the safety of those inside the cars than those riding or walking outside them. The fallout studies probed the dangers of contaminated milk to readers of *Consumer Reports*, not the dangers of radioactivity to the world.[14]

The studies undertaken here, however, indicate that through product testing, Consumers Union did considerably more than reinforce conventional consumer behavior. The unique strength of the organization's approach lay in its ability to plant its calls for reform in the evidence of practical problems and personal risks. The reports cited in this study in fact helped to expose the difficulty of protecting public health in the face of ingrained habits of smoking and an intransigent tobacco industry; they helped to exert a measure of control over the automobile industry for the sake of public safety; they helped the government and the public to develop greater awareness of radioactive dangers to the environment.

Consumers Union played a pioneering role in other areas as well. *Consumer Reports* publicized the dangers of pesticides in the food chain well before the publication of Rachel Carson's book *Silent Spring*. The organization published studies about the cost of air pollution to consumers, and about chemicals and dangerous additives in foods. Consumers Union considered the problems of safe and effective methods of birth control. These explorations and many others extended the definition of consumer interests beyond a narrow or selfish outlook. They established a base for the most important domestic reform issues of the Nixon, Ford, and Carter years.[15]

By the early 1970s, Consumers Union had become the organization that many had hoped it would be from the beginning: reputable, scientific, and influential. In 1974 the director of communications at Consumers Union, Ira Furman, described sending a memo that indicated the new sense of having arrived:

A year ago, I sent a memo around to everyone telling them we finally made it because the *Wall Street Journal* referred to us as Consumers Union, period—not "Consumers Union of the U.S.,

a nonprofit organization. . ." Well, I was joking, you know, but
everyone knows who we are now . . . and we don't really need
anyone looking over our shoulders. We do enough looking over
our own shoulders.

Consumers Union had begun with an aspiration to respectability and
power. It also had begun with an idealistic, radical sense of mission. At
first, the scientific method it appropriated conveyed radical political and
economic lessons. By the close of the Second World War, the lessons and
the sense of mission had softened.[16]

Method came to determine the scope of mission in the pages of
Consumer Reports. Prudence, impartiality, and scientific objectivity became the hallmark of Consumers Union. Within CU, the staff had become less ideologically focused and more professionally capable. Without,
a large readership had come to trust CU and to expect guidance about the
culture of consumption.

There is a Japanese legend about an actor who wore the same mask
every day for many years. One day, when the actor took the mask off, he
discovered that his face had taken on the same appearance as the mask.
The mask had reformed the actor, yet to the world the actor's image
looked quite the same. Like that actor, Consumers Union had been transformed by its own method and its own history, while its outer appearance
remained unchanged.

Appendix

A TABULATION OF THE MAIL received by the Reader's Service section of Consumers Union provides some indication of the interest that *Consumer Reports* provoked in the controversies about smoking and auto safety. The number of incoming requests for information about those problems and about products related to those problems, expressed as a proportion of the total number of requests, is taken as a measure of this interest. The

TABLE 1

Requests for Information Concerning Smoking and Auto Seat Belts

	Total Number of Requests	Requests about Cigarettes	Computed Proportion, Cigarettes	Requests about Seat Belts	Computed Proportion, Seatbelts
1945	1,553	0	0	0	0
1946	5,639	21	.00372	0	0
1947	8,209	13	.00158	0	0
1948	10.013	10	.00099	0	0
1949	9,031	0	0	0	0
1950	10,521	0	0	0	0
1951	8,114	0	0	0	0
1952	9,550	11	.00115	0	0
1953	12,247	46	.00375	0	0
1954	11,840	42	.00355	0	0
1955	7,674	16	.00209	0	0
1956	8,398	20	.00238	29	.00345
1957	8,473	14	.00165	12	.00142
1958	11,229	31	.00276	10	.00089
1959	10,986	47	.00428	16	.00146
1960	10,430	30	.00288	70	.00671
1961	9,262	14	.00151	102	.01101
1962	8,226	20	.00243	107	.01300
1963	7,286	14	.00192	108	.01482

actual number of letters received was never large, but proves statistically significant and represents an underlying trend. The pertinent data are reported in Table 1. The proportions are charted in Figures 1 and 2.

Comparable data are available for the years 1945–1963. The total number of requests that were recorded by the Reader's Service during those years ranged from 1,553 to 12,247. Since many different kinds of requests for automotive information were included in the tabulations prepared by the Reader's Service, only requests for information about seat belts are included in Figure 1. Included in the computation of the proportions exhibited in Figure 2 are requests for information about tobacco, cigarettes, or antismoking devices.

From Figure 1 it is clear that nonzero proportions occur only after 1955. In Figure 2, the proportions after 1953 are sustained at a higher

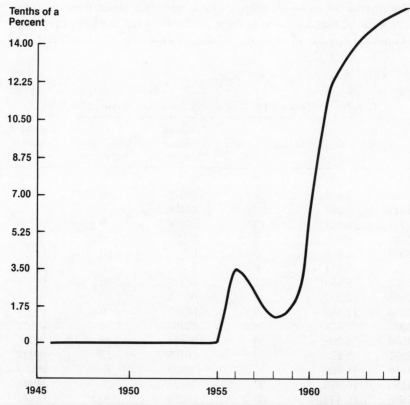

FIGURE 1. Volume of requests from readers of *Consumer Reports* for information about seat belts, 1945–1963, expressed as a percentage of all requests for information coming to the Reader's Service of Consumers Union.

FIGURE 2. Volume of requests from readers of *Consumer Reports* for information about cigarettes, 1945–1963, expressed as a percentage of all requests for information coming to the Reader's Service of Consumers Union.

**Tenths of a
Percent**

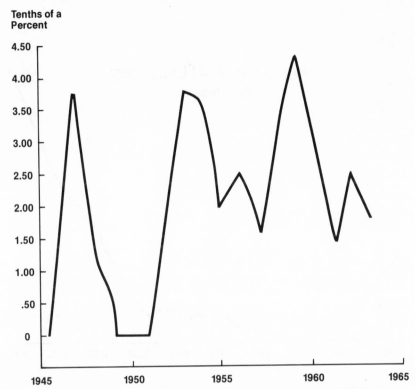

level than during the years before that date.* The number of requests in any year was affected by many factors besides the reporting of Consumers Union, including inquiries provoked by commercial advertising and other sources of information. The combined effect of all sources of information, however, was to increase the proportion of the readership that was concerned about smoking and about safety belts between 1945 and 1963.

The data show that the proportion of letters written to Consumers Union relating to the controversies about smoking and auto safety was reaching higher levels with the progression of years. Assuming that those who wrote to the magazine to ask for advice did so because they took

---

*If a single proportion is computed for all the years before 1953 combined, and another for the years after that date, then standard statistical tests of the difference between the two proportions indicate that the difference is highly significant. The Chi² statistic with one degree of freedom is 68, and a T statistic takes the value of 9.5.

seriously the evaluations and views appearing in *Consumer Reports,* the growing proportions support the position that Consumers Union played an increasingly important role for its readers in the two controversies during this period.

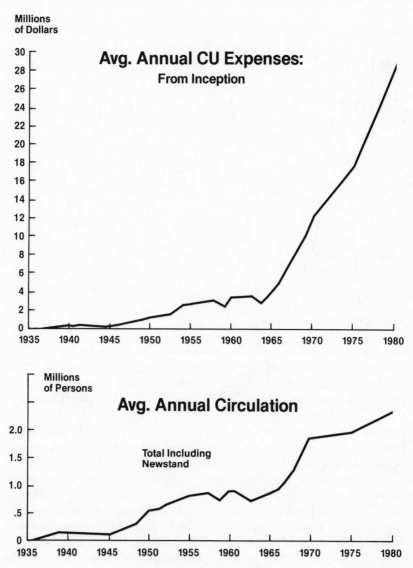

FIGURE 3.   From information provided by Consumers Union

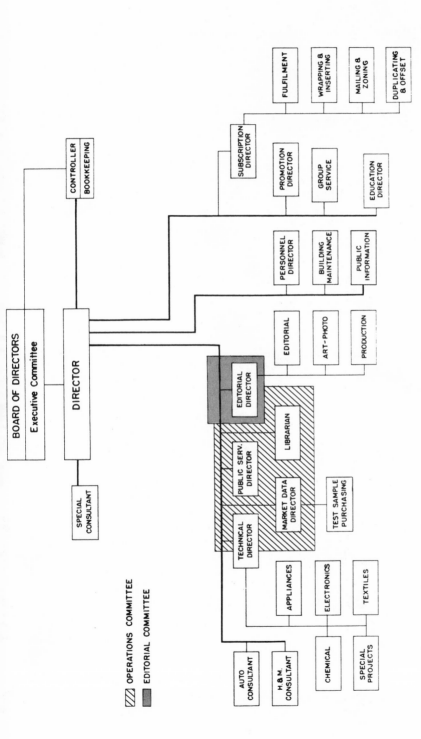

FIGURE 4.   Consumers Union Staff Functions and Organization January 1962

Notes

Preface

*For a discussion of the internal history of Consumers Union, see Norman Katz, "Consumers Union, the Movement and the Magazine, 1936–1957" (Rutgers University, Ph.D. thesis, 1977).

CHAPTER I

The Tradition of Consumer Protest

1. Frederick J. Schlink, "Safeguarding the Consumers' Interest: An Essential Element in National Recovery," address delivered at the Conference on Progress toward National Recovery, American Academy of Political and Social Sciences, January 6, 1934, located at the Center for the Study of the Consumer Movement (hereafter CSCM). About the difficulties of mobilizing to defend a "consumer interest," see Mancur Ohlson, *The Logic of Collective Action* (Cambridge, Mass., 1971).

2. Robert Lynd, "The Problem of the Consumer," *Annals of the American Academy of Arts and Sciences*, May 1936, 1–7; Dora Weiner, "Public Health During the French Revolution," delivered to the Yale History Department, February 15, 1974; E. P. Thompson, "The Moral Economy of the English Crowd," *Past and Present*, February 1971, 76–136.

3. Lydia Maria Child, *The American Frugal Housewife* (Boston, 1835); Katherine Kish Sklar, *Catherine Beecher* (New Haven, 1973), 151–155, 164–167.

4. Daniel Boorstin, *The Americans: The Democratic Experience* (New York, 1973), 193–199; Earl P. Stevenson, "Scatter Acorns that Oaks May Grow: Arthur D. Little, Inc., 1886–1953" (New York, Newcomen Society, 1953); Harry Chase Brearly, *A Symbol of Safety* (Garden City, New York, 1923), 30; Rexmond C. Cochrane, *Measures for Progress: A History of the National Bureau of Standards* (Washington, D.C., Department of Commerce, 1966), 14.

5. Cochrane, *Measures*, 90–102.

6. Boorstin, *Democratic Experience*, 434–49; Boorstin, *The Image: A Guide to Pseudo-Events in America* (New York, 1961), 181–238.

7. Otis Pease, *The Responsibilities of American Advertising: Private Control and Public Influence* (New Haven, 1958), chapters 1–4; Laura Wertheimer, "From Protection to Deception: The Transmogrification of the Good Housekeeping Seal of Approval" (unpublished Yale College seminar paper), CSCM; Peter Samson, "The Emergence of a Consumer Interest in America," (University of Chicago, Ph.D. thesis, 1980), 8–47.

8. See Richard B. Fisher, "The Last Muckraker: The Social Orientation of the Thought of Upton Sinclair" (Yale University, Ph.D. thesis, 1953); Oscar E. Anderson, *The Health of a Nation: Harvey Wiley and the Fight for Pure Food* (Chicago, 1958), 172–196.

9. Wesley C. Mitchell, "The Backward Art of Spending Money," *American Economic Review*, June 1912, 269–281.

10. Helen Sorenson, *The Consumer Movement* (New York, 1941), 3–157; Peter Samson, "Emergence of a Consumer Interest," 37–44; L. H. Bailey, *The Country Life Movement in the United States* (New York, 1915), 58–76; George Rosen, *Preventative Medicine in the United States in Historical Perspective*, statement prepared for the National Conference on Preventative Medicine, June 1975; Walter Lippmann, *Drift and Mastery* (New York, 1914), 52–56; Ronald Steel, *Walter Lippmann and the American Century* (New York, 1980), 74–89.

11. Cochrane, *Measures*, 177–178.

12. Special issue devoted to standardization, *Annals of the American Academy* May 1928, 47.

13. Albert W. Whitney, "The Place of Standardization in Modern Life," *Annals of the American Academy of Arts and Sciences*, May 1928, 32–39; Frederick Schlink and Robert Brady, "Standards and Specifications from the Standpoint of the Ultimate Consumer," *Annals of the American Academy of Arts and Sciences*, May 1928, 231–240; see also Ruth O'Brien, "Consumers Lose Confidence in Brands Because of Lack of Quality Standards," *Industrial Standardization and Commercial Standards Weekly*, December 1934, 269; Robert Lynd, "Why the Consumer Wants Quality Standards," *Advertising and Selling*, January 4, 1934, 15; P. G. Agnew, "Technical Standards for Consumer Goods—A 'Five-Year Plan'?," *Journal of Home Economics*, December 1931, 1095; C. R. Palmer, "Why Buying by Brand Is Better than by Specification," *Printer's Ink*, January 18, 1934, 70.

14. P. G. Agnew, "Twenty Years of Standardization," *Industrial Standardization*, October 1938, 229; Herbert Hoover, chairman, American Engineering Council on the Elimination of Waste in Industry of the Federated American Engineering Societies, *Waste in Industry* (New York, 1921), 1–33.

15. Thorstein Veblen, *The Theory of the Leisure Class* (New York, 1899); Edward Bellamy, *Looking Backward* (Boston, 1887), Signet edn., 157.

16. Stuart Chase, *The Challenge of Waste* (New York League for Industrial Democracy, 1922); Chase, *Technocracy: An Interpretation* (New York, 1933); Chase, *The Tragedy of Waste* (New York, 1925); Robert B. Westbrook, "Tribune

of the Technostructure: The Popular Economics of Stuart Chase," *American Quarterly*, Fall 1980; and interviews of Chase by Norman Silber, September 29, October 7, 18, 1977, Oral History Collection (hereafter OHC), CSCM.

17. John Bates Clark, *Essentials of Economic Theory as Applied to Modern Problems of Industry and Public Policy* (New York, 1907), esp. 1–20, 39–58; Simon Patten, *The Consumption of Wealth* (University of Pennsylvania, 1889), 2; Daniel Horowitz, "Consumption and its Discontents: Simon Patten, Thorstein Veblen, and George Gunton," *Journal of American History*, September 1980, 301–307.

18. Lippmann, *Drift and Mastery*, 52–56.

19. Pease, *Responsibilities*, 20–33.

20. Veblen, *Absentee Ownership*, 306; Stuart Chase and Frederick Schlink, *Your Money's Worth* (New York, 1927), 9.

21. Pease, *Responsibilities*, 22.

22. *Historical Statistics of the United States, Colonial Times to 1957* (Washington, D.C., Department of Commerce, 1960), series F 1–5, 131; Robert Lynd, "The People as Consumers," *Recent Social Trends in the United States, Report of the President's* [Hoover] *Research Committee on Social Trends* (New York, 1933), II, 857–911.

23. For example, Studs Terkel, *Hard Times* (New York, 1970), esp. 44–76, 198–227.

24. Veblen, *The Engineers and the Price System* (New York, 1921), 9.

25. *Consumers' Research General Bulletin*, July 1933, 15; E. B. White, "The Urgency of an Agency," *New Republic*, April 1, 1931; *Consumers' Research General Bulletin*, July 1933, 15; Colston E. Warne, "The Case Against Advertising," *Annals of the American Academy of Arts and Sciences*, May 1936, 15.

26. Bellamy, *Looking Backward*, 72.

27. Maud Nathan, *The Story of an Epoch-Making Movement* (New York, 1926); John Elliott Ross, *Consumers and Social Reform* (New York, 1912), 23; Sorenson, *The Consumer Movement*.

28. Alice Rosenberg Wolfe, "Women, Consumerism, and the National Consumers' League in the Progressive Era," *Journal of Labor History*, Summer 1975, 384–392; *Consumers Union Reports* (hereafter *CR*), November 1937; April 1938.

29. "Beatrice and Sidney Webb," supplement to *New Statesman*, May 8, 1915; also Beatrice and Sidney Webb, *The Consumers' Cooperative Movement* (London, 1921); Seba Eldridge, "Socialism Via the Consumers: From Private Ownership to Public Control," *Common Sense*, February 1934, 19–23; Bertram Fowler, *Consumer Cooperation in America: Democracy's Way Out* (New York, 1936); E. J. Lever, "A New Appeal for the Cooperative Movement," *Cooperation*, April 1932; Harold Loeb, "Consumer Action: A Neglected Weapon," *Common Sense*, June 1935, 16–19.

30. Persia Campbell, *Consumer Representation in the New Deal* (New York, 1940), 31; John Chamberlain, "Who Is the Consumer?," *Common Sense*, June 1934, 15–16.

31. Arthur Feiler, "The Evolution of the Consumer," *Annals of the American Academy of Arts and Sciences*, March 1938, 1–8; Frederick Schlink, letter to the Editor, *Common Sense*, August 1934, 15–16.

CHAPTER II

Consumer Reform as a Science

1. Stuart Chase and Frederick Schlink, *Your Money's Worth* (New York, 1927).
2. Sybil Schwartz Shainwald, "The Genesis and Growth of the First Consumer Product Testing Agency," (Columbia University, M.A. thesis, 1971), 47–81, CSCM; *Consumers' Research Bulletin* promotional flyer, undated, Consumers' Research pamphlet material, CSCM.
3. Arthur Kallet and Frederick Schlink, *100,000,000 Guinea Pigs* (New York, 1933.)
4. The guinea-pig genre of literature included: M. C. Phillips, *Skin Deep* (New York, 1934); James Rorty, *Our Master's Voice—Advertising* (New York, 1934); Frederick Schlink, *Eat, Drink and Be Wary* (New York, 1935); Arthur Kallet, *Counterfeit—Not Your Money But What It Buys* (New York, 1935); J. B. Matthews, *Guinea Pigs No More* (Washington, New Jersey, 1935); J. B. Matthews and J. E. Shallcross, *Partners in Plunder* (New York, 1935); Walter B. Pitkin, *Let's Get What We Want* (New York, 1935); E. Jerome Ellison and Frank W. Brock, *The Run for Your Money* (New York, 1935); Bissell Palmer, *Paying Through the Teeth* (New York, 1935); Rachel Palmer and Sarah Greenberg, *Facts and Frauds in Women's Hygiene* (New York, 1936); Peter Morrell, *Poisons, Potions and Profits* (New York, 1937); George Seldes, *Lords of the Press* (New York, 1938); Ruth Brindze, *Not to Be Broadcast—The Truth About Radio* (New York, 1937); Rachel Palmer and Isadore Alpher, *40,000,000 Guinea Pig Children* (New York, 1937); Elizabeth Hawes, *Fashion Is Spinach* (New York, 1938). Replies to the guinea-pig authors were also numerous, including G. L. Eskew, *Guinea Pigs and Bug-Bears* (New York, 1938), and Frank Dalton O'Sullivan, *The Poison Pen of New Jersey* (Chicago, 1936). Among the most popular and balanced contemporary discussions of food and drug problems was *The American Chamber of Horrors* written by Ruth DeForrest Lamb (New York, 1936). See William Stott, *Documentary Expression and Thirties America* (New York, 1973), 152–189.
5. *Consumers' Research Bulletin*, general series, 1928–1936; Frederick Schlink, "What the Government Does and Might Do for the Consumer," *Annals of the American Academy of Arts and Sciences*, May 1934.
6. Schlink, "What Government Does," *op. cit.*; see also *Consumers' Research Bulletin*, 1928–1936.
7. "Buyers' Baedeker," *New Republic*, November 26, 1930, 32; "In the Driftway," *Nation*, April 8, 1931, 380; Stuart Chase, "Consumers' Tomorrow," *Scribner's*, December 1933, 333–338; *Survey Graphic*, February 1934, 71–75. Sponsors of Consumers' Research in 1933 included: labor organizer and pacifist

A. J. Muste; Isador Lubin of the Brookings Institution; educator Henry Harap; Harry Laidler, executive director of the League for Industrial Democracy; Edward Lindeman of the New School for Social Research; historian Harry Elmer Barnes; Norman Thomas; and economists Edith Ayres, Robert Brady, Paul Douglas, Fred Fairchild, Dexter Keezer, Frank Knight, Sumner Slichter, Rexford Tugwell, Colston Warne, and W. F. Willcox.

8. Schwartz Shainwald, "Genesis and Growth," 159 –183; Arthur Kallet, "Partners in Strike-Breaking: Consumers as Workers vs. Consumers as Employers," *Common Sense*, October 1935, 22; Consumers' Research Strike Material, Colston E. Warne Collection, CSCM; "Later Strike Developments at CR," *Consumers' Research Bulletin*, October 1935, 18–24.

9. *Nation*, September 25, 1935, 636; *New York Times*, September 9, 1935, 2:8; January 14, 1936, 2:3; January 29, 1936, 25:2; *Business Week*, October 12, 1935, 30.

10. Schwartz Shainwald, "Genesis and Growth," 148–183; Niebuhr Committee, "Report on the Strike at Consumers' Research," CSCM; National Labor Relations Board Report, Second Region, Case No. II–C–24, "In the Matter of Consumers' Research," Consumers' Research Strike Materials, CSCM.

11. "Later Strike Developments," *op. cit.*; Joseph B. Matthews, *Odyssey of a Fellow-Traveler* (New York, 1938); Consumers Union Board Minutes (hereafter CUBM), May 25, 1936, and September 27, 1937; *CR*, May 1936, inside cover.

12. Sponsors of Consumers Union as of March 4, 1936: Robert S. Allen, Willard E. Atkins, Jacob Baker, Sam Baron, Edward Berman, Paul Blanshard, S. John Block, Louis Boudin, Leroy E. Bowman, Leonard Bright, Mrs. James Campbell, Winifred Chappell, Malcolm Cowley, Mary Ware Dennett, Carl Dreher, Robert Dunn, Walter Frank, Varian Fry, Mrs. Kate Crane Gartz, Elisabeth Gilman, Dr. Abraham Goldforb, Francis Gorman, Mrs. J. C. Guggenheimer, Louis M. Hacker, Mathilde Hader, Herbert C. Hanson, Henry Harap, Abraham L. Harris, Benjamin Harrow, Albion Hartwell, Aline Davis Hays, Arthur Garfield Hays, Julius Hochman, Darlington Hoopes, Quincy Howe, Rabbi Edward Israel, Gardner Jackson, Calvin Johnson, Matthew Josephson, Horace M. Kallen, Allen Kennan, Harold Loeb, Grace Lumpkin, Robert S. Lynd, Ernest L. Meyer, Clyde Miller, William J. Murphey, Gardner Murphy, Vincent J. Murphy, Theodore Newcomb, William Nunn, Harry A. Overstreet, Paul Peterson, Evelyn Preston, Leslie Preston, Mrs. Jacob Riis, I. M. Rubinow, George Seldes, Theodore Shedlovsky, Mrs. Datus C. Smith, I. W. Soper, Anna Louise Strong, Clinton J. Taft, Lewis M. Terman, Max Trumper, Marion S. Van Liew, Harold Ward, Goodwin Watson, Helen Woodward, Leane Zugsmith.

For information about the grant, see Consumers Union Treasurer's Report, 1937, exhibit B, CSCM; also Katz, "Consumers Union," Chapter III.

13. CUBM, May 25, 1936, and September 27, 1937; Eugene Beem, "Consumer Testing and Rating Agencies in the United States," (University of Pennsylvania, Ph.D. thesis, 1951), 126–130; CUBM, March 5, 1937.

14. *CR*, 1936–1939; see interviews between Colston Warne, Sybil Schwartz Shainwald and Dewey Palmer, April 26, 1970, OHC, CSCM; of Dr. Harold Aaron by Norman Silber, August 12, 1975, OHC, CSCM; of Edward Brecher by Norman Silber, September 16, 1975, OHC, CSCM.

15. Correspondence from Dewey Palmer to Paul Williams, U.S. Department of Agriculture; to Foster D. Snell, Inc.; to food processing companies, Food Test Project File, Consumers Union Library; see also *CR*, 1936–1939.

16. *CR*, May 1938, 10; CUBM, October 26, 1938; February 7, 1939; November 12, 1939.

17. Colston E. Warne, "The Relationship of the Consumer Movement to Scientific Groups," speech delivered to a meeting of the American Association for the Advancement of Science, read before the American Association of Scientific Workers, December 30, 1939, CSCM; *Science in the Service of the Consumer, Proceedings of the Fourth Annual Meeting of Consumers Union . . . ,"* June 17, 18, 1940, CSCM; CUBM, July 17, 1940, Advertising and Editorial Files (hereafter AEF), CSCM.

18. Federated Press Release, June 2, 1939, AEF, CSCM; Gallup finding in Beem, "Consumer Financed," 117; *CR*, June 1937, 32; "Members Report," *CR*, October 1939, 8–9.

19. George Seldes, *Lords of the Press* (New York, 1938), 384–392; *CR*, January–February 1937; August 1939; Colston E. Warne, "Consumer Action Programs of the Consumers Union of the United States," in Ralph M. Gaedeke and Warren E. Etcheson, *Consumerism* (San Francisco, 1972); *CR*, December 1937, 2; January 1939, 17.

20. U.S. House of Representatives, Special Subcommittee of the Committee to Investigate Un-American Activities, 75th Congress, 3rd Session (Dies Committee), "Testimony of J. B. Matthews," December 3, 1939; Report of the Joint-Fact-Finding Committee to the Fifty-fifth California Legislature, "Un-American Activities in California," Sacramento, 1943, Jack B. Tenney, Chairman, 100–104, CSCM; CUBM, January 10, 1940; J. B. Matthews, *Odyssey of a Fellow Traveler*.

21. *Bread and Butter*, February 25, 1941–March 29, 1947 (weekly); CUBM, April 15, 1945.

22. CUBM, February 27, 1944; April 15, 1945; June 1, 1948.

23. Technical Inquiries (Reader's Service tabulations), 1945, CSCM; circulation data from the Office of the Associate Director, Consumers Union, 1971, extrapolation from Schwartz Shainwald, "Genesis and Growth," appendices.

24. CUBM, June 1, 1948; October 18, 1949; September 27, 1950; Beem, "Consumer Financed," 145.

25. Interview of Colston E. Warne by Sybil Schwartz Shainwald, October 21, 1971, OHC, CSCM; CUBM, December 23, 1947; August 1, 1951; *CR*, 1949–1953; "TRB," *New Republic*, September 21, 1953, AEF, CSCM; Harry Hollins, Bakersfield, California, *Union Labor Journal*, January 18, 1951, AEF, CSCM.

26. *CR*, 1948–1953; CUBM, August 15, 1951.

27. Consumers Union of the United States, Inc., against Frank J. Walker, Postmaster General of the United States, U.S. Court of Appeals for the District of Columbia, #8704; appeal of decision in District Court, January 21, 1944; Consumers Union of the United States, Inc., against Doeskin Products, Inc., and Henry B. Cohen Advertising Company, Inc., defendants, U.S. District Court, Southern District, March 1, 1950; Federal Trade Commission Complaint 5800, August 17, 1950, "In the Matter of Doeskin Products, Inc.," Legal Cases Files, CSCM; see also *Nation*, June 24, 1939; *Printer's Ink*, July 28, 1939, clippings files,

Legal Cases, CSCM; on labor, *New York World Telegram*, July 11, 1952, CSCM; ad agency, *Space and Time* (New York City) July 17, 1950, AEF, CSCM; labor, CUBM, February 27, 1951; clearance CUBM, March 20, 1953; purchase, *CR*, September 1954, 394.

28. Interview of Irving Michelson by Norman Silber, July 11–25, 1974; of Colston Warne by Sybil Shainwald, July 1972; of Paul Kern and Colston Warne by Sybil Shainwald, February 1972, OHC, CSCM; *Time*, August 12, 1957.

29. William H. Whyte, Jr., "The Consumer in Modern Society," paper presented at the Institute for Consumer Problems (sponsored by Consumers Union), University of Minnesota, July 18–20, 1955; "Researchers' Best Test Is Often a Small Boy," *New York Times*, November 30, 1959, AEF, CSCM.

30. For example: Hugh Williams Sargent, "The Influence of Consumer-Product Testing and Reporting Services on Consumer Buying Behavior" (University of Illinois, Ph.D. thesis, 1958); Harry L. Strickling, "Implications of the Existence of Consumers Union for Marketers of Major Appliances and Related Consumer Durables" (New York University, M.B.A. thesis, 1965); Ruby Turner Morris, "Consumers Union: Methods, Implications, Weaknesses and Strengths" (published privately, 1971), CSCM; Joyce Oliver Rasdall, "Product Information as a Resource: A Study of the Factors Affecting Its Usefulness to Consumers" (Ohio State University, Ph.D. thesis, 1973).

31. William Rossi, "The Economics of Needs and Wants," *Leather and Shoes*, February 5, 1955, AEF, CSCM; parodies included *Jackpot*, "Consumer Report on Girls," December 1957, 17–19ff; *Humbug*, November 1957, "*Consumer Retorts*; best buys in confetti, seismographs, rickshaws," 23–27; *Frantic*, February 1959; "*Cornsumer Reports*, Complete ratings of bubblegum, portable and unportable portables"; *Mad*, "*Condemner Reports*," January 1970, AEF, CSCM.

32. "Report on an address by Frederick Wickert, Michigan State University," *Lansing State Journal*, February 3, 1960, AEF, CSCM.

33. "Report of Technical Policy Committee, 1958," Sidney Margolius, chairman, Board Committees Files, CSCM; "Report of the Technical Policy Committee," October 24, 1959, William Pabst, chairman, Board Committees Files, CSCM; Robert A. Brady, "The Status, Functioning and Prospects of Consumers Union," August 24, 1956, CSCM.

34. Robert Lynd, "Consumers Union Anniversary Comments," 1961, CSCM; Colston E. Warne, "Address to Members, Twenty-fourth Annual Report," June 17, 1961, CSCM.

CHAPTER III

The Risk of Smoking: Verifying
the Tradition of Temperance

1. Interview of Colston E. Warne by Norman Silber, July 31, 1975, OHC, CSCM; *CR*, 1936–1980.

2. Robert K. Heimann, *Tobacco and Americans* (New York, 1960), 6;

Jerome E. Brooks, *The Mighty Leaf* (New York, 1952), 245; Joseph C. Robert, *The Story of Tobacco in America* (New York, 1949), 3–16.

3. Henry Gibbons, M.D., *Tobacco and Its Effects, a Prize Essay Showing that the Use of Tobacco is a Physical, Mental, Moral and Social Evil* (New York, 1868), 30–36, Yale University Medical Library Historical Collection (hereafter YUML); Orin Fowler, *A Disquisition on the Evils of Using Tobacco* (1842), YUML.

4. Moses Stuart, in A. McAllister, *Dissertation on the Medical Properties of the Habitual Use of Tobacco* (Boston, 1830) YUML; Reverend Benjamin Ingersol Lane, *Responses on the Use of Tobacco* (New York, 1846), YUML; Joel Shew, *Tobacco: Its History, Nature and Effects on the Body and Mind* (New York, 1849), 32–36, YUML; George Trask, *The Anti-Tobacco Journal* (1859), Arents Tobacco Collection, New York Public Library (hereafter NYPL).

5. McAllister, *Dissertation*, 24; Shew, *Tobacco*, 36; Margaret Lawrence (Meta Lander, pseudonym), *The Tobacco Problem* (Boston, 1886), 24–37; *Lancet* citation in Lee Fritschler, *Smoking and Politics* (New York, 1969), 6; R. D. Mussey, *An Essay in the Influence of Tobacco Upon Life and Health* (American Tract Society, 1836), 11–64, YUML.

6. Lander, *Tobacco Problem*, 59–170; Gibbons, *Tobacco and Its Effects*, 24–25; George Trask, "Anti-Tobacco Literature," pamphlet file, Arents Collection, NYPL.

7. Heimann, *Tobacco and Americans*, 90–94; Benno K. Milmore and Arthur G. Coxover, "Tobacco Consumption in the United States, 1880–1955," *Agricultural Economic Research*, VIII, January 1956, 9–13.

8. Jerome Brooks, *The Mighty Leaf*, 249.

9. Joseph Robert, *Story of Tobacco*, 245–254; Lawrence, *Tobacco Problem* (sixth edition), Arents Collection, NYPL, 119–180; N. A. Hunt, *Tobacco Manual* (Portland, Maine, 1888), Arents Collection, NYPL.

10. Joseph Robert, *Story of Tobacco*, 250–265; Brooks, *The Mighty Leaf*, 253; Lawrence, *The Tobacco Problem*, 83–96; H. W. Farnam, "Our Tobacco Bill: A Tentative Social Balance Sheet" (New York, 1914); Joseph Robert, *Story of Tobacco*, 138–154.

11. Twymon O. Abbott, "The Rights of the Non-Smoker," *The Outlook*, April 2, 1910; Lucy Gaston Page, in *Life and Health*, XXII, 380–387; Austin v. Tennessee, 179 U.S. 343; 21 Sup. Ct. 132; 45 L.Ed. 224; see also 144 N.W. 661; 193 Pac. 347.

12. Henry Ford, *The Case Against the Little White Slaver* (Detroit, 1916), YUML; Luther Burbank, "Tobacco, Tombstones and Profits," *Dearborn Independent*, July 21, 1923; John Harvey Kellogg, *Tobaccoism, or How Tobacco Kills* (Battle Creek, Michigan, 1922), 120–131; M. V. O'Shea, *Tobacco and Mental Efficiency* (New York, 1923).

13. Hiemann, *Tobacco and Americans*, 250–251; Kellogg, *Tobaccoism*, 120–131.

14. O'Shea, *Tobacco and Mental Efficiency*, v–ix.

15. Susan Wagner, *Cigarette Country* (New York, 1971), 42–47; Edward Brecher and the Editors of *Consumer Reports*, *Licit and Illicit Drugs* (Mount Vernon, New York, 1972), 230–233.

16. Milmore and Coxover, "Tobacco Consumption," 9–13; Daniel H. Kress, M.D., *The Cigarette as a Physician Sees It* (Mountain View, California, 1931), 52–53; Edward L. Bernays, *Biography of an Idea: Memoirs of Public Relations Counsel Edward L. Bernays* (New York, 1965), in Warren Susman, *Culture and Commitment* (New York, 1973), 133–141.

17. Interview of Edward Brecher by Norman Silber, September 16, 1975, OHC, CSCM; of Irving Michelson by Norman Silber, March 7, 1974, OHC, CSCM;, *CR*, July 1938, 5–9.

18. Jessie Coles, *The Consumer Buyer and the Market* (New York, 1938), 44–49; A. E. Hamilton, *This Smoking World* (New York, 1927), 181–182.

19. This and the following paragraph refer to *CR*, November 1937, 13; "Cigarettes-Brands," project test file, Consumers Union Library.

20. Colston E. Warne, "The Challenge of the Consumer Movement," *Social Action*, December 15, 1940, 1–25; *CR*, July 1938, 5–9.

21. Edith Ayres, "Private Organizations Working for the Consumer," *Annals of the American Academy*, May 1934, 158.

22. This and the following paragraphs refer to *CR*, July 1938, 5–9; "Cigarettes-Brands," project test file, Consumers Union Library.

23. *CR*, July 1938, 5–9; "Cigarettes-Brands," project test file, Consumers Union Library; interview of Alexander Crosby by Norman Katz, November 19, 1974, OHC, CSCM.

24. *CR*, July 1938, 5–9; August 1938, 18–19.

25. This and the following paragraphs refer to *CR*, July 1938, 5–9.

26. Interview of Edward Brecher by Norman Silber, September 16, 1975, OHC, CSCM.

27. Richard B. Tennant, *The American Cigarette Industry* (New Haven, Connecticut, 1950), 115–174; Joseph Robert, *The Story of Tobacco in America*, 261–265.

28. *CR*, September 1941, 229–232; U.S. v. American Tobacco Company, et al., District Court, Eastern District of Kentucky, July 24, 1940, in *Temporary National Economic Committee Monograph*, XXI, 1940.

29. *Business Week*, November 8, 1941, 17–18; July 11, 1942, 58.

30. Tennant, *American Cigarette Industry*, 115–179.

31. Gene Tunney, "Nicotine Knockout, or the Slow Count," *Reader's Digest*, December 1941, 21–24; *Business Week*, August 17, 1942, 24.

32. *CR*, July 1942, 171; *Reader's Digest*, July 1942, 5–8.

33. *CR*, July 1942, 171; April 1943, 106; September 1943, 249.

34. *CR*, September 1942, 228; July 1947, 274; September 1947, 328; May 1950, 189; Ruth and Edward Brecher, Arthur Herzog, Walter Goodman, Gerald Walker, and the Editors of *Consumer Reports, The Consumers Union Report on Smoking and the Public Interest* (Mount Vernon, New York, 1963), 145.

35. Interview of Irving Michelson by Norman Silber, March 7, 1974, OHC, CSCM; *CR*, August 1941, 207; July 1945, 117.

36. *CR*, 1946–1949; Ballot Questionnaire analysis, CSCM; see also interview of Dr. Harold Aaron by Norman Silber, August 12, 1975, OHC, CSCM.

37. R. Pearl, "Tobacco Smoking and Longevity," *Science*, March 4, 1938, 216; *Smoking and Health, Report of the Advisory Committee to the Surgeon*

General of the Public Health Service (U.S. Department of Health, Education and Welfare, Washington, 1964), 139–155; *Time*, November 30, 1953, AEF, CSCM.

38. *Smoking and Health*, 139–155; Little, cited in Harold Diehl, *Tobacco and Your Health* (New York, 1969), 21.

39. Alton Ochsner, M.D., "Relationship of Cigarette Smoking to Lung Cancer," reprinted in "False and Misleading Advertising (Filter-tip Cigarettes)", hearings before a Subcommittee of the House Committee on Government Operations of the Eighty-fifth Congress (Blatnik Subcommittee), July 18–26, 1957, 407; interview of Dr. Harold Aaron by Norman Silber, August 12, 1975, OHC, CSCM; *CR*, March 1948, 124, 131.

40. *CR*, March 1948, 123; interview of Dr. Harold Aaron by Norman Silber, August 12, 1975, OHC, CSCM.

41. *Ibid.*

42. *CR*, January 1949, 35.

43. R. H. Rigdon, M.D., "Consideration of the Relationship of Smoking to Lung Cancer," *Southern Medical Journal*, April 1957, 524–533; Ernest A. Wynder, M.D., "Place of Tobacco in the Etiology of Lung Cancer," *Cancer of the Lung: An Evaluation*, Proceedings of Scientific Session, Annual Meeting of the American Cancer Society, November 3–4, 1953, 29–36.

44. *Smoking and Health*, 149–210; Wynder, "Place of Tobacco in the Etiology of Lung Cancer," 29–36.

45. E. L. Wynder, E. A. Graham, and A. B. Croninger, "Experimental Production of Carcinoma with Cigarette Tar," *Cancer Research*, XIII, 855–864, 1953.

46. Roy Norr, "Cancer by the Carton," *Reader's Digest*, December 1952, 7–8; "Smoke Gets in the News," *Life*, December 21, 1953, 20–21.

47. *CR*, February 1954, 54; February 1955, 67; Tobacco Industry Research Committee, *Report(s) of the Scientific Director*, 1956–1961; citation in 1956 report, 23.

48. George Gallup, *The Gallup Poll* (New York, 1972), November 1, 1949, 874; Milmore and Coxover, "Tobacco Consumption," 9–13.

49. *CR*, February 1955, 61–63.

50. *CR*, February 1953, 63–65.

51. *CR*, February 1955, 54; Herbert Brean, *How to Stop Smoking* (New York, 1951).

52. This and the next paragraphs refer to an interview of Irving Michelson by Norman Silber, March 7, 1974, OHC, CSCM.

53. *CR*, June 1952, 262.

54. *CR*, February 1953, 59–74; February 1955, 57–73; March 1957, 100–110; September 1957, 406–409; October 1957, 460–462; November 1957, 542–543; January 1958, 24–25; February 1958, 92–93; March 1958, 126–127; April 1958, 224–225; December 1958, 628–636; January 1960, 13–21; April 1961, 203–207; June 1963, 265–281.

55. *CR*, March 1957, 107–110.

56. *CR*, 1958–1963; March 1957, 100.

57. Mildred Brady, "Testimony before the Federal Trade Commission on

Proposed Trade Regulations Governing the Future Advertising and Labeling of Cigarettes," March 18, 1964, mimeo, CSCM.

58. *New York Times,* February 4, 1953, AEF, CSCM; *New York World Telegram,* February 4, 1953, AEF, CSCM; *Magazine Digest,* May 1953, AEF, CSCM; Dr. Walter Alvarez, syndicated column, distributed June 19, 1953, AEF, CSCM; *Top Secret,* August 1955, AEF, CSCM; *Advertising Age,* January 24, 1955, AEF, CSCM.

59. CUBM Director's Report, September 20, 1960.

60. Milmore and Coxover, "Tobacco Consumption," 913; Vance Packard, *The Hidden Persuaders* (New York, 1957), 43; *CR,* March 1957, 102.

61. *Consumers Union Report on Smoking and the Public Interest,* 31–37; Gilliam in *CR,* February 1955, 69.

62. *CR,* February 1955, 69; Dr. Charles S. Cammeron, "Lung Cancer and Smoking," *Atlantic,* January 1956, 75.

63. *CR,* May 1957, 250; George Gallup, *The Gallup Poll,* July 21, 1957, 1501; *Smoking and Health, a Summary and Report of the Royal College of Physicians of London* (London, 1962).

64. "False and Misleading Advertising (Filter-tip Cigarettes)," 1–309.

65. *CR,* April 1958, 224–225.

66. *CR, ibid.; Time,* March 3, 1958, 78.

67. *New York Times,* July 27, 1957, 19; Fritchler, *Smoking and Politics,* 24–25; *Washington Evening Star,* July 24, 1957, AEF, CSCM; Albany, Oregon, *Democratic Herald,* March 7, 1957, AEF, CSCM; *Group Health,* March 1957, number 2, 14.

68. Fritchler, *Smoking and Politics,* 24–25; Susan Wagner, *Cigarette Country,* 81.

69. *CR,* December 1958, 631.

70. "Umpiring the Cigarette Ad Claims: The Methods and Ethics of Testing Labs," *Printer's Ink,* July 4, 1958, 56; *New York World Telegram,* February 24, 1958, 3; "CU Tobacco Fact Sheet," *Vend* (Chicago), April 1958, AEF, CSCM; Consolidated News Feature Release, "Trade Winds," April 6, 1958, AEF, CSCM; *Advertising Age,* March 3, 1958, AEF, CSCM; letter from Colston E. Warne to Commissioner John W. Gwynne, Federal Trade Commission, August 19, 1957, Consumers Union Library.

71. *Time,* March 31, 1958, 79; "Cigarette Test Project Expenditure Request," CUBM Executive Committee Minutes, July 18, 1958, CSCM.

72. Irving Michelson, "The Chemist's Ethics and the Community," *The Chemist,* January 1962, Michelson Collection, CSCM; Ian Fleming, *Thunderball* (London, 1961), 65.

73. Press Release, Radio and Newspaper Publishers' Distributing Corporation, May 1959, AEF, CSCM; interview of Irving Michelson by Norman Silber, March 7, 1974; Mildred Brady, "Testimony before Federal Trade Commission," March 18, 1964, CSCM.

74. *Publishers' Weekly,* July 8, 1963, 154; Brecher Collection, smoking material, CSCM; Ruth and Edward Brecher, et al., *Smoking and the Public Interest,* 173–211.

75. *Smoking and the Public Interest;* Edward P. Morgan, *AFL–CIO News,* September 7, 1963, AEF, CSCM; "Excerpts from Early Comments on the *Consumers Union Report on Smoking and the Public Interest,*" Brecher Collection, smoking material, CSCM, *New York Times,* July 17, 1963, AEF, CSCM; *New York Times Book Review,* October 20, 1963; William Styron, "The Habit," *New York Review of Books,* December 26, 1963; "The Drive for the Teen-age Market," *PTA,* October 1963, 23; *Presbyterian Life,* October 17, 1963, AEF, CSCM; *Christianity Today,* November 8, 1963, AEF, CSCM.

76. *Variety,* July 31, 1963, 36, AEF, CSCM; *Kansas City Star,* July 21, 1963, AEF, CSCM; *Saturday Review,* August 10, 1963, 52; August 24, 1963, 38; *Television,* August 1963, AEF, CSCM; *Newsweek,* July 29, 1963, letter to editor, CSCM; *The New Republic,* September 21, 1963, 15.

77. Brecher Collection, smoking material, CSCM; *Wall Street Journal,* November 12, 1963, 22.

78. Sen. Maurine Neuberger, *Smoke Screen: Tobacco and the Public Welfare* (Englewood Cliffs, New Jersey, 1963), 49–66; Ruth and Edward Brecher, et al., *Smoking and the Public Interest,* 173–211; Thomas Whiteside, "A Cloud of Smoke," *New Yorker,* November 30, 1963, 67–77.

79. Interview of Edward Brecher by Norman Silber, September 16, 1975, OHC, CSCM.

80. *CR,* May 1976, 278; *The Health Consequences of Smoking* (U.S. Department of Health, Education and Welfare, 1974), esp. vii–x.

81. *Ibid.*

82. Edward Brecher and the Editors of *Consumer Reports, Licit and Illicit Drugs* (Mount Vernon, New York, 1972).

CHAPTER IV

Accidents and Injuries: Testing
the Automobile Industry

1. *CR,* June 1936, 3; quotation in *CR,* May 1953, 182; see also interview of Dewey Palmer by Sybil Shainwald, April 26, 1970; interview of Colston Warne by Norman Silber, July 31, 1975, OHC, CSCM.

2. Dewey H. Palmer and Laurence E. Crooks, *Millions on Wheels* (New York, 1938), 8; *CR,* May 1953, 219.

3. *CR,* May 1936–November 1966.

4. James J. Flink, *America Adopts the Automobile, 1895–1910* (Cambridge, Mass., 1970), 64–70 (hereafter *America*); James J. Flink, *The Car Culture* (Cambridge, Mass., 1975), 18–22; John Rae, *The American Automobile* (Chicago, 1965), 29–32; "Evolution of the Motor Car Has Been Meteoric," *New York Times* supplement, January 14, 1914.

5. Keith Sward, *The Legend of Henry Ford* (New York, 1948), 5–6 (hereafter *Ford*); Flink, *America,* 181–193 (*Outlook* citation on 181); Robert A. Wolf

and John C. Fralish, "A Brief History of Motor Vehicle Accident Investigation," *Proceedings of the Collision Investigation Methodology Symposium*, August 24–28, 1969, Department of Transportation Library (hereafter DOT).

6. *Report of the Philadelphia Bureau of Highways*, 1911; Lewis Mumford, *The Highway and the City* (New York, 1963), 234–246.

7. Flink, *America*, 70–112; Sward, *Ford*, 32–45; "Evolution," *New York Times*, January 14, 1914; *Historical Statistics of the United States: Colonial Times to 1970* (Washington, U.S. Department of Commerce, 1975), series Q148–162, 716, (hereafter *Historical Statistics*).

8. William Phelps Eno, *The Story of Highway Traffic Control, 1899–1939* (Eno Foundation, Conn., 1939), citation p. 59; Wolf and Fralish, "Brief History,"; Flink, *America*, 165–195; Flink, *Car Culture*, 25–28.

9. Flink, *America*, 165–195.

10. *Historical Statistics*, series Q224–232, 720.

11. Wolf and Fralish, "Brief History"; Flink, *America*, 113–128.

12. American Museum of Safety, *Safety* (New York, published irregularly 1919–1936); National Congress for Industrial Safety, *Proceedings* (Chicago, published irregularly, 1914–present).

13. "Evolution," *New York Times* supplement, January 14, 1914; Flink, *Car Culture*, 166.

14. *Historical Statistics*, series Q224–232, 720; Flink, *Car Culture*, 165.

15. Wolf and Fralish, "Brief History"; *Reports of the First National Conference on Street and Highway Safety* (Washington, Department of Commerce, 1924–1925), vols. 1–8, citation vol. 1, p. 7.

16. *First National Conference; Reports of Second National Conference*, March 23–25, 1926 (Washington, Department of Commerce, 1926).

17. Committee Report on the Motor Vehicle, *First National Conference*, December 1, 1924; Flink, *Car Culture*, 165.

18. George Thompson, "Intercompany Technical Standardization in the Early American Auto Industry," *Journal of Economic History*, Winter 1954; "Safer Cars," *Literary Digest*, November 14, 1936.

19. "Ten Commandments of Safe Driving," *School Life*, December 1936; Ralph Nader, *Unsafe at Any Speed: The Designed-in Dangers of the American Automobile* (New York, 1965), Pocket Books edn., 176–177.

20. J. C. Furnas, "AND SUDDEN DEATH," *Reader's Digest*, August 1935; "—and sudden death," *Literary Digest*, January 18, 1936.

21. The Gallup Poll (New York, 1972), 12; Franklin D. Roosevelt, "A New Year's Message," *Reader's Digest*, January 1936.

22. Stuart Chase and Frederick Schlink, *Your Money's Worth* (New York, 1927); see also *Consumers' Research Bulletin*, issues for 1929.

23. Chase and Schlink, *op. cit.*, 3, 78.

24. Interview of Dewey Palmer by Sybil Shainwald, Colston Warne, and Sidney Shainwald, April 26, 1970, OHC, CSCM.

25. Palmer, *op. cit.*; interview of Laurence Crooks by Colston Warne and Sybil Shainwald, June 1970, OHC, CSCM.

26. D. H. (Dewey) Palmer, "Automobile Safety Before Beauty," *Consumers'*

Research Bulletin, July 1933, 10–11; "Buying an Automobile by Specification," *Consumers' Research Bulletin*, June 1935, 19–20.

27. *CR*, June 1936, 3.

28. *Ibid*.

29. Palmer and Crooks, *Millions on Wheels*, 3–16.

30. *Ibid.*, Palmer and Crooks, *op. cit.*, 18, 288.

31. CUBM, October 26, 1938; November 12, 1939; *CR*, May 1950, 190.

32. *CR*, February 1942, 38; June 1942, 47; August 1943, 206; September 1943, 259.

33. *CR*, August 1946, 199; May 1948, 197; interview of Fred Wood by Norman Silber, August 1977, OHC, CSCM; see also automotive test project technical reports, 1948–1960, CSCM.

34. A. Howard Hasbrook, "The Historical Development of the Crash-impact Engineering Point of View," in William Haddon, Edward Suchman and David Klein, eds., *Accident Research: Methods and Approaches* (Harper and Row, 1964, hereafter *Accident Research*); Hugh DeHaven, "Accident Survival— Airplane and Passenger Automobile," paper presented at January 1952 meeting of SAE, reprinted in Haddon, Suchman and Klein, *Accident Research*.

35. DeHaven, "Accident Survival," *op cit*.

36. Ibid.

37. Wolf and Fralish, "Brief History"; John P. Stapp, "Human Tolerance to Deceleration," in Haddon, Suchman and Klein, *Accident Research*; Verne L. Roberts, "Motor Vehicle Restraints," in International Safety Conference Compendium, 978–993, DOT; John O. Moore and Boris Tourin, "A Study of Automobile Doors Opening Under Crash Conditions," ACIR project study, August, 1954.

38. *CR*, May 1946, 116; May 1948, 201; February 1948, 72; May 1950, 195; October 1950, 453; May 1952, 217; May 1953, 195; exchange of letters between Colston E. Warne and T. P. Wright, vice-president, Cornell University, November 28, 1952, October 5, 1953, Colston E. Warne Collection, CSCM; CUBM, December 4, 1952.

39. "Safer Accidents," *Time*, October 19, 1953; "Built-in Safety?," *Business Week*, May 1, 1954; "How We Can Have Safe Cars," *Colliers*, January 10, 1953.

40. *CR*, May 1953, 218; Jean Whitehill, "Women's Dollars in Today's Market," *Newsdealer*, April 1952, AEF, CSCM; Consumers Union News Release, April 16, 1953, AEF; Racine, Wisconsin, *Journal-Times*, May 22, 1954, AEF, CSCM.

41. *CR*, May 1955, 214; "Safety Drive Penetrates Public Apathy," *Casualty-Bonding*, January 2, 1954, AEF; Donald C. Lhotka, "The Seat Belt Story," *Traffic Safety*, November 1964, 22–35: *Hearings Before the House Subcommittee on Health and Safety of the Interstate and Foreign Commerce Committee*, July 7–9, 1959, 88–89; *The Gallup Poll*, 1360; *Historical Statistics*, series Q163–174; Charlotte, N.C. *News*, November 18, 1953, AEF, CSCM.

42. *CR*, May 1955, 214.

43. *Gallup Poll*, 1349; "The Seat Belt Story," 22–35; John D. States, "Passenger Protection in Automobiles: A Medical Problem with a Legal Solution," DOT reference copy.

44. Robert H. Fredericks, "Ford Motor Company Research in Delethalization," in *Passenger Car Design and Highway Safety* (Mount Vernon, New York, 1962), 205–215; *Newsweek,* March 5, 1956, 57; *Newsweek,* March 19, 1956, 62; Ralph Nader, *Unsafe at Any Speed,* 88–93.

45. *CR,* April 1956, 168.

46. *CR,* May 1956; Director's Report to Board, March 15, 1961, 4, CSCM; interview with Irving Michelson by Norman Silber, March 23, 1974; test project file on seat belts, CSCM.

47. *CR,* May 1956, 212–217.

48. *New York Post,* June 3, 1956, AEF, CSCM; news release, Publishers' Distributing Corporation, May 1, 1956, AEF; letter to Consumers Union from Sergei Feitelberg, concerning report of seat-belt tests in German auto magazine, AEF; *Bulletin of the American College of Surgeons,* July–August 1956, AEF; *Hearings of the House Subcommittee on Traffic Safety of the Committee on Interstate and Foreign Commerce,* June 1956; *New York Times,* August 19, 1956, AEF, CSCM.

49. Lhotka, "Seat Belt Story," 22–35; Nader, *Unsafe at Any Speed,* 90.

50. Lhotka, *op. cit.,* 23; Nader, *op. cit.,* 91.

51. *CR,* April 1956, 145–208; May 1956, 212.

52. *CR,* January 1955, 9; October 1957, 472; interview of Fred Wood by Norman Silber, August 1977; "Racing for Safety," *Sports Illustrated,* October 19, 1959, 48–55; Accountant's Report to the Board of Directors, year ending May 31, 1949, 53; Treasurer's Report Number One to Board of Directors, year ending May 31, 1958.

53. *CR,* April 1957, 145–208.

54. Laurence E. Crooks, "New, Smaller Cars Will Come From Behind in Handling, Steering," *SAE Journal,* July 1959, 28–29; *Hearings Concerning Administered Prices Before the Senate Committee on Anti-trust and Monopoly,* April 29, 1958, 3067–3089; *CR,* July 1958, 351.

55. *CR,* April 1959, 175.

56. *CR,* August 1958, 411; interview with Irving Michelson by Sybil Shainwald and Norman Silber, March 28, 1974, OHC, CSCM; *CR,* July 1962, 344; *CR,* November 1962, 527; letters from George Goss to CEW, September 1958, Colston E. Warne Collection, CSCM; States, "Passenger Protection in Automobiles," DOT reference.

57. Irving Michelson, Bertil Aldman, Boris Tourin and Jeremy Mitchell, "Dynamic Tests of Restraining Devices for Automobile Passengers," *Public Health Reports,* February 1964; reviewed in *Traffic Safety,* February, 1963, AEF. The participants in the conference were: James Stannard Baker, director of research and development, Traffic Institute, Northwestern University; Irwin D. J. Bross, Department of Biostatistics, Roswell Park Memorial Institute; B. J. Campbell, Automotive Crash Injury Research Center; Harry C. Doane, assistant to the vice-president, the General Motors Engineering Staff; Richard G. Domey, Harvard School of Public Health; Edward R. Dye, consulting engineer; John C. Fitch, associate, Cornell Aeronautical Laboratories and Lime Rock proving ground; Robert H. Fredericks, Ford Engineering and Research Staff; John W.

Garrett, Cornell Crash Injury Research; James L. Goddard, Federal Aviation Agency (former head of Accident Prevention Program at U.S. Public Health Service); William Haddon, director, Epidemiology Residency Program, New York State Department of Public Health; Roy Haeusler, automotive safety engineer, Chrysler Corporation; Herbert H. Jacobs, Dunlap and Associates; Robert N. Janeway, president, Janeway Engineering Company; Francis P. Lowrey, Auto Industries Highway Safety Committee; Myron I. Macht, Automotive Crash Injury Research; John G. Manikas, traffic safety representative, Ford Motor Company; Alexander V. Monto, chief, traffic safety, U.S. Public Health Service; John Moore, director of research and development, American Safety Equipment Corporation; Daniel P. Moynihan, special assistant to Secretary of Labor Arthur J. Goldberg; Lee Rainwater, Social Research, Inc.; Edwin M. Schechter, Dunlap and Associates; Robert J. Schreiber, Public Service Research, Inc.; Leonard Segel, Cornell Aeronautical Laboratory; William F. Sherman, Automobile Manufacturers Association; William I. Stieglitz, chief, Design Safety and Reliability, Republic Aviation Corporation; John E. Ullman, Department of Management, Hofstra College; William H. Wandel, Nationwide Insurance Company; Robert A. Wolf, director, Automotive Crash Injury Research.

58. *CR*, August 1961, 467; April 1963, 184; see chapter 5, "Fallout in Food."

59. Grant materials, Michelson Papers, CSCM.

60. Lhotka, "Seat Belt Story," 22–35; Paul Kearney, "How Safe Are the New Cars?" *Harper's*, February 1957; Daniel P. Moynihan, "Epidemic on the Highways," *Reporter*, April 30, 1959; see also Nader, *Unsafe at Any Speed*, 59.

61. For example: Associated Press Release, April 30, 1958, AEF; Associated Press Science Service release, June 15, 1959, AEF; *Printer's Ink*, June 27, 1958, AEF; Publishers' Distributing Corporation, Press Release, February 18, 1960, AEF; Amarillo, Texas *News*, January 31, 1960, AEF; *Automotive News*, February 1, 1960, AEF; Escanaba, Michigan *Press*, October 19, 1961, AEF; *Automotive Market Report*, March 31, 1958, AEF; Tampa, Florida *Independent*, July 3, 1959, AEF; Flint, Michigan *Review*, June 18, 1959, AEF; *New York Times*, April 30, 1958, 22; Nashville *Tennessean*, May 1, 1958, AEF; Lawrence, Massachusetts *Eagle*, May 1, 1958, AEF; *Business Week*, May 3, 1958, AEF; *Automotive News*, May 5, 1958, AEF; Tulsa *Tribune*, June 30, 1958, AEF; according to the Annual Report of the Director, October 18, 1958, CSCM, the Dreyfuss article alone was reported in more than 100 newspapers and magazines.

62. *CR*, October 1961, 546.

63. *Report of the Joint Committee on Motor Vehicles and Traffic and Highway Safety*, New York State Legislature (Albany, Legislative Document Series, 1961).

64. Lothka, "Seat Belt Story," 22–35; "State Legislatures in Scramble to Enact Seat Belt Laws," *SAE Journal*, Technical Section, 1964, DOT reference; U.S. Congress, Public Law 88–515, 1963.

65. *CR*, April 1965, 168; David Klein and William Haddon, "The Prospects for Safer Autos," *CR*, April 1965, 176.

66. Nader, *Unsafe at Any Speed*; Charles McCarry, *Citizen Nader* (Signet,

1972), 13–75; Thomas Whiteside, *The Investigation of Ralph Nader* (Arbor House, 1972), 11–23.

67. Interview of Irving Michelson by Sybil Shainwald and Norman Silber, March 28, 1974, OHC, CSCM; CUBM, April 11, 1967; *CR*, February 1966, 84–91; April 1966, 194–197.

68. *CR*, April 1966, 161; *The Gallup Poll*, 828; U.S. Congress, Public Laws 89–563 and 89–564, 1966.

69. Consumers Union, *Passenger Car Design and Highway Safety*, v; *CR*, May 1966, 258; interview with Colston Warne by Norman Silber, July 31, 1975, OHC, CSCM.

70. Palmer and Crooks, *Millions on Wheels* (New York, 1938).

71. John Burby, *The Great American Motion Sickness* (Mount Vernon, New York, 1971).

CHAPTER V

Fallout in Food: Exposing Environmental Contamination

1. "The Milk We Drink," *CR*, March 1959, 102–111; Lawrence Wittner, *Rebels Against War: The American Peace Movement, 1941–1960* (New York, 1969), 240; Eugene J. Rosi, "Mass and Attentive Opinion on Nuclear Weapons Tests and Fallout, 1954–1963," *Public Opinion Quarterly*, summer 1965, 286–288; see Robert A. Divine, *Blowing on the Wind: The Nuclear Test Ban Debate* (Oxford, 1978).

2. Divine, *op. cit.*, 3–35.

3. *Ibid.*

4. Wittner, *Rebels*, 240–256; Harold Karan Jacobson and Eric Stein, *Diplomats, Scientists, and Politicians, the United States and the Nuclear Test Ban Negotiations* (Ann Arbor, 1966), 20; Ralph Lapp, "The 'Humanitarian' H-bomb," *Bulletin of Atomic Scientists*, September 1956, 264; Divine, *Blowing on the Wind*, 82.

5. "One Scientist Speaks Up," *Science*, December 31, 1954, 5A; "Atomic Clouds Over America," *Science Digest*, June 1953, 23–30; "Assuring Public Safety in Continental Weapons Tests," *Bulletin of Atomic Scientists* (hereafter *BAS*), April 1953, 85–89; "H-bomb Contamination," *Science Newsletter*, May 28, 1955, 345; "H-bomb and the Great Unsolved Problems," *BAS*, May 1954, 146 ff; "Fallout and Candor," *BAS*, May 1955, 170ff; "Still in the Dark on Radiation Danger," *Christian Century*, June 1, 1955, 645; *New Republic*, April 4, 1955, 23; "Death in the Rain," *Nation*, August 6, 1955, 111–114; "Are Atomic Tests Dangerous?" *Reporter*, April 7, 1955, 23; *Science Newsletter*, February 26, 1955, 205; "Contamination of the Earth's Atmosphere," *New Yorker*, March 19, 1955, 29.

6. Jacobson and Stein, *Diplomats*, 24–25; Divine, *Blowing on the Wind*, 94; Rosi, "Mass and Attentive Opinion," 286–288; Hazel Gaudet Erskine, "The Polls:

Atomic Weapons and Nuclear Energy," *Public Opinion Quarterly,* summer 1963, 184–189.

7. Divine, *Blowing on the Wind,* 126, 160, 165; Wittner, *Rebels,* 240–256; Earl H. Voss, *Nuclear Ambush, The Test Ban Trap* (Chicago, 1962), 93–135; Mary Milling Lepper, *Foreign Policy Formulation, A Case Study of the Nuclear Test Ban Treaty of 1963* (Columbus, Ohio, 1971), 18–67.

8. Lepper, *op. cit.*

9. Notes of Irving Michelson, "from a panel discussion at Argonne National Laboratory," June 9, 1958, located in Radiation Projects Papers, CSCM; Michelson to J. Laurence Kulp, April 28, 1959, Radiation Papers, CSCM; Michelson to Dexter Masters, "planning session," April 9, 1959; Michelson memo, "present status of Public Service Projects Department," October 15, 1959, Irving Michelson Papers, CSCM; Correspondence, April–June 1958, Radiation Papers, CSCM.

10. Michelson and Masters personnel files, CSCM.

11. Correspondence, April–June 1958, Radiation Papers, CSCM; *CR,* September 1958, 458ff; Michelson memo to Morris Kaplan, CU technical director, and Dexter Masters, concerning trip to Washington, May 28, 1958, technical file, Strontium 90 in Milk, CSCM; correspondence, April–June 1958, Radiation Papers, CSCM.

12. Strontium 90 technical file, CSCM.

13. Raw work sheets; Michelson memo to Kaplan, June 9, 1958, strontium 90 technical file, CSCM.

14. Interview of Irving Michelson by Sybil Shainwald, March 21, 1974; John M. Fowler, *Fallout, a Study of Superbombs, Strontium-90 and Survival* (New York, 1960).

15. Market Research Corporation of America, profile of dairy products, in *Advertising Age,* October 19, 1959, 72.

16. Michelson, "Outline for Report," November 14, 1958; first draft of "Milk We Drink," Strontium Technical File, CSCM; "Excerpts from letters on the Sr-90 in Milk Report," Radiation Papers, CSCM; *Hearings, Joint Committee on Atomic Energy, Subcommittee on Radiation,* III (May 5, 6, 7, 8, 1959), 2167–2169.

17. *CR,* March 1959, 102–111.

18. *Op. cit.,* 103, 111.

19. "Report to Editorial," March 17, 1959; correspondence, March–June, 1959, Radiation Papers, CSCM; "Some Developments in the Wake of CU's Fallout Report," *CR,* May 1959, 262–263; see AEF, CSCM.

20. *New York Post,* February 20, 1959; *St. Louis Post-Dispatch,* March 2, 4, 1959; *Washington Post* and *Times-Herald,* March 7, 1959; *Quebec Chronicle-Telegraph,* March 10, 1959; *Norfolk Ledger-Dispatch,* March 27, 28, 1959; *Journal of the American Medical Association,* April 18, 1959, 40; *Brotherhood of Maintenance of Way Employees Journal,* May, 1959; *Dog World,* April 1959, AEF, CSCM.

21. *CR,* February 1959; Ernest B. Kellogg to CU, January 21, 1959, Radiation Papers, CSCM; U.S. Department of Agriculture, Economic Research Service, *The Dairy Situation,* November 12, 1962, 1ff; "Dairy Men Hone Ad Weapons for Cholesterol War," *Advertising Age,* April 3, 1961, 100.

22. Tables, "Average Daily Receipts of Milk from Producers in Various Mar-

keting Areas" and "Average Daily Sales of Whole Milk," U.S. Department of Agriculture, *Fluid Milk and Cream Report*, May 1959 and June 1960; Kellogg to CU, March 18, 1959; Kaplan to Kellogg, March 25, 1959; Kellogg to Kaplan, April 2, 1959, Radiation Papers, CSCM.

23. John F. Corcoran, "Public Service Campaign Combats Fears about Fallout in Milk," *Public Relations Journal*, July 1962, 37–38.

24. *Farm Journal*, July 1959, 13; Corcoran, 37–38; William K. Wyant, Jr., "Strontium-90 in St. Louis," *Nation*, June 13, 1959, 536; "Some Developments," *CR*, May 1959, 262; letters from New York State Department of Health, March 24, 1959; Massachusetts Department of Health, April 2, 1959; *La Moure Chronicle* (North Dakota), January 26, 1960, AEF; Isotopes, Inc., May 1, 1959, Radiation Papers, CSCM.

25. *New York Times*, March 8, 1959, 32; Walter Schneir, "A Primer on Fallout," *Reporter*, July 9, 1959, 17–24; Walter Schneir, "Strontium-90 in U.S. Children," *Nation*, April 25, 1959, 355–357; *Hearings, Joint Committee on Atomic Enery, Subcom. Radiation* (May 5, 6, 7, 8, 1959, 1961, 1953–1959, 1968).

26. "Primer," *Reporter*.

27. *Ibid.; New York Times*, April 25, 1959, 5.

28. "Primer," *Reporter;* 73 U.S. Statutes at Large 688, "An Act to Amend the Atomic Energy Act of 1954, as Amended. . . ," S. 2568, September 23, 1959.

29. Erskine, 184–189; addition to testimony of Irving Michelson, *Hearings, Joint Committee on Atomic Energy,* June 3, 1960.

30. Michelson planning session memo, April 8, 1959, and Michelson to James Terrill, assistant chief of Radiological Health Division, PHS, January 13, 1961; Michelson memo regarding proposed contest, April 7, 1960, Radiation Papers; correspondence with Greater St. Louis Nuclear Information Committee, Radiation Papers, CSCM.

31. Michelson memo, October 15, 1959; memo to Board of Directors, October 14, 1959, Michelson Papers, CSCM; *CR*, June 1960, October 1961, March, April 1962.

32. Warne, letter to radiation field-workers, May 6, 1965, Radiation Papers, CSCM; *Hearings, Joint Committee on Atomic Energy, Subcom. Radiation* (May 5, 6, 7, 8, 1965), 1940ff; Michelson to Flemming, January 22, 1960, Radiation Papers, CSCM; "Strontium-90 in the Total Diet," *CR*, January 1960, 5–6; "Fallout in Our Milk . . . a Follow-up Report," *CR*, February 1960, 64–70; *CR*, June 1960, 289–293.

33. *CR*, September 1960, back cover; August 1961.

34. "Give Us the Truth About Fallout," *Christian Century*, November 22, 1961, 1387; "If You're Worried About Fallout," *U.S. News*, October 2, 1961, 93–95; "Test's Aftermath: Hot Cargo," *Time*, November 3, 1961, 49.

35. *CR*, October 1961; January 1962.

36. Dairy Council of California, *Focus*, January 1962; Letter from C. K. Johns, Canada Department of Agriculture, Dairy Technology Research Institute, February 26, 1962; letter from A. C. Dahlberg, Department of Dairy Science, Cornell University, February 2, 1962; letter from E. A. Perregaux, executive director, Connecticut Milk for Health, January 19, 1962, Radiation Papers, CSCM.

37. Release, Milk Industry Foundation, January 8, 1962; *Santa Rosa* (Calif.) *Press* feature section, January 7, 1962, Radiation Papers, CSCM; Quotation in letter from Bishop and Associates, public relations representatives for National Dairy Council, January 25, 1962, CSCM; *CR*, January 1962.

38. "The Nutritional Significance and Safety of Milk and Milk Products in the National Diet," release, National Academy of Sciences, National Research Council, May 25, 1962, Consumers Union Library; Corcoran, "Public Service Campaign," 37–38; Rosi, "Mass and Attentive Opinion," 286–288; Wittner, *Rebels*, 240–256.

39. Rosi, *op. cit.*

40. *Hearings, Joint Committee on Atomic Energy* (June 5, 1962); *New York Times*, August 18, 1962, 19; *CR*, January 1962, 8.

41. "Iodine in Fallout: A Public Health Problem," *CR*, September 1962, 446–447; *New York Times*, July 5, 1962, 5.

42. "Fallout 1963, an Interim Report," *CR*, September 1963, 448–449.

43. Ad Hoc Dose Assessment Group, Nuclear Regulatory Commission, "Population Dose and Health Impact of the Accident at Three Mile Island Nuclear Station (preliminary assessment for March 28–April 7, 1979)," May 10, 1979, 74–77.

CHAPTER VI

Science and Reform

1. Colston E. Warne, "Address to the Twenty-fourth Annual Meeting," July 17, 1961, CSCM.

2. Max Lerner, *America as a Civilization* (New York, 1957), 209; specialized treatments include Mary O. Furner, *Advocacy and Objectivity* and *Crisis in the Professionalization of American Social Science* (Lexington, Ky., 1975); Edward A. Purcell, *The Crisis of Democratic Theory: Scientific Naturalism and the Problem of Value* (Lexington, Ky., 1973).

3. Harold Orlans, *The Non-Profit Research Institute* (Berkeley, 1972), 3–39; Charles B. Saunders, Jr., *The Brookings Institution, A Fifty-Year History* (Washington, D.C., 1966), 38; about Marxism and science, see Maurice Cornforth, *The Open Philosophy and the Open Society* (New York, 1968), I.

4. Jacques Barzun in Banesh Hoffman, *The Tyranny of Testing* (New York, 1962), introduction.

5. Colston E. Warne, in *Annals of the American Academy of Political and Social Sciences*, May, 1934; Malinda Berry Orlin, "The Consumer Needs a Thousand Eyes, the Buyer Only One" (University of Pittsburgh, Ph.D. thesis, 1973), 248.

6. Interesting in this regard is Robert A. Brady, "The Status, Functioning and Prospects of Consumers Union," August 24, 1956, CSCM.

7. See Robert Lynd, "Consumers Union Anniversary Comments," 1961, CSCM; David Riesman, *Abundance, for What?* (New York, 1964).

8. For example, letters to the editors in monthly issues of *CR;* also Jack Engledow, "The Impact of *Consumer Reports* Ratings on Purchase Behavior and Post-Purchase Product Satisfaction" (Indiana University, Ph.D. thesis, 1971), 36–41.

9. John Dewey, "The Supremacy of Method," from *The Quest for Certainty* (New York, 1929), in Milton Konvitz and Gail Kennedy, *The American Pragmatists* (New York, 1960), 191.

10. Nader cited in Elin Schoen, "*Consumer Reports* Knows What's Best for Us All," *Esquire*, February 1974, 108–111ff.

11. Alvin Gouldner, *The Coming Crisis of Western Sociology* (New York, 1970), 103; *CR*, May 1936, back cover.

12. Schoen, "*Consumer Reports* Knows," *op. cit.*; Herbert Marcuse, *One-Dimensional Man* (Boston, 1964), 9.

13. *CR*, September 1975, 524–526; sales of subscriptions reported to *Ayer Directory of Publications* (Bala Cynwyd, Pa., 1970–1980).

14. See chapters III, IV, V in this book.

15. *CR*, May 1937, 27; 1938, 24; (air pollution) July 1957, 344; August 1960, 285; (food additives) March 1950, 135; (contraceptives) see "CU Report on Contraceptives," special publication, 1937, 1939, CSCM.

16. Schoen, "*Consumer Reports* Knows," *op. cit.*

Bibliographical Essay

THIS BOOK DEPENDED on many sources, including manuscripts, archival records, government publications, journals, and books. The freedom that Consumers Union extended to me to review and quote from its records made this research possible.

The opportunities for exploring consumer protest and the social history of consumer technology were enlarged in 1973, when the National Endowment for the Humanities helped to establish the Center for the Study of the Consumer Movement (CSCM) at the headquarters of Consumers Union. The core of the Center's records relate to the history of Consumers Union since 1936. Some internal records are lost, but the remaining material includes several hundred manuscript and file boxes, encompassing minutes of the board of directors, committee papers, office and technical files, official statements and testimony, financial reports, ballot questionnaires, speeches, Reader's Service tabulations, legal records, reports of the executive director, memoranda relating to consumer conferences, grants, anniversary celebrations, and research collections assembled by the staffs of different departments and divisions. Chapters 2, 3, and 4 and the case studies in this book relied especially on project files concerning radiation hazards, methods of testing cigarettes, and the work of the Auto Test facility. Advertising and editorial files, containing news clippings about the work of Consumers Union, indicated the influence in print of *Consumer Reports*.

The Center also holds documents from individual consumer advocates and organized consumer groups. Records of the National Association of Consumers, the Intermountain Consumers' Service, and the International Organization of Consumers Unions, while not cited in the notes, provided information about alliances of consumer groups and the development of international consumer affairs. The personal papers of Colston E. Warne illuminated anti-advertising sentiment, the Consumers' Research strike, the development of Consumers Union, and other aspects of consumer protest. The papers of Henry Harap helped to trace the development of consumer education, aspects of the history of home economics, and the development of consumer standards. The papers of Irving Michelson, Morris Kaplan, Edward Brecher, Paul Kern, and Leland Gordon supplemented institutional records and shed light on the case studies. The Consumers Union Library and its Staff Information Services kindly made available correspondence between Consumers Union and government agencies, and provided access to files bearing on relations between CU and its outside consultants.

I also appreciate the courtesies and assistance afforded me by the librarians of Yale and Columbia universities, Sarah Lawrence College, and the New York Public Library Research Collection.

The Arents Collection of Tobacco Literature of the New York Public Library (New York City) contains a unique selection of books and special materials about the history of tobacco, including the opposition to smoking. I also located nineteenth- and twentieth-century antismoking tracts in the History of Medicine Collection at the library of the Yale University School of Medicine. To learn about recent health questions related to smoking, I used materials at the offices of the *Medical Letter* in New Rochelle, New York. The National Milk Producers' Institute (Washington, D.C.) permitted me to review records of its activity during the controversy about strontium 90 in milk.

The reference library of the Environmental Protection Agency (Washington, D.C.) and the National Clearinghouse on Smoking and Health (Atlanta, Georgia) provided pamphlet material about the radiation and smoking controversies, which included documents obtained from predecessor groups. The computerized bibliographic services of the Department of Transportation library (Washington, D.C.) offered proceedings of conferences and papers about automotive safety that would have been otherwise inaccessible.

The National Archives (Washington, D.C.) held the scattered files of the Consumer Advisory Board of the National Recovery Administration (Record Group 9, Office File of the Special Advisor to the Consumer Advisory Board), the Consumers' Division of the Office of Price Administration (Record Group 188, Office of the Consumer Relations Adviser, 1941–1947), and the Consumer's Division of the National Emergency Council (Record Group 44, Correspondence of the Consumers' Division, 1934–1935). At the Manuscript Division of the Library of Congress, I researched the extensive papers of the National Consumers League. The Stuart Chase Collection, also within the Manuscript Division, yielded information about Consumers' Research and the origin of product testing.

Federal congressional proceedings, published in Washington, D.C., included *Hearings of the U.S. Temporary National Economic Committee,* Thurman Arnold, chief investigator (Monograph #21, 1940, 76th Congress, 3rd session, Senate Committee print), and *Investigation of Un-American Propaganda Activities in the United States,* Martin Dies, Chairman (August 12–December 14, 1939, 1938–1939, 75th Congress, 3rd session, v. I–IV).

Regarding the problem of smoking, I consulted *Hearings on False and Misleading Advertising (Filter-tip Cigarettes), Subcommittee of the House Committee on Government Operations,* John Blatnik, chairman (July 18–26, 1957, 85th Congress, 1st session). Concerning fallout in food, I found the *Hearings of the Joint Committee on Atomic Energy* to be essential. See *Effect on Health, Safety and Weather of Atomic Explosions,* Clinton P. Anderson, chairman (April 15, 1955, 84th Congress, 1st session); *Radioactive Fallout, Effects on Man,* Carl T. Durham, chairman (May 27–June 7, 1957, 85th Congress, 1st session); *Radiation Protection Criteria and Standards: Their Basis and Use,* Chet Holifield, chairman (May 1960, June 1961, 87th Congress, 1st session); *Radiation Standards, Including Fallout,* Chet Holifield, chairman (September 1962, 87th Congress, 2nd session); and *Fallout, Radiation Standards and Countermeasures,* John O. Pastore, chairman (June 3–August 27, 1963, 88th Congress, 1st session). Regarding automobile safety, see *Reports of the First National Conference on Street and Highway Safety* (Department of Commerce, 1924–1925, v. I–VIII); *Automobile Seatbelts, Hearings of the Traffic Subcommittee of the House Interstate and Foreign Commerce Committee,* Kenneth Roberts, chairman (April 30–August 8, 1957, 85th Congress, 1st session); *Hearings Concerning Administered Prices (Automobiles), Senate Subcommittee on Anti-Trust and Monopoly of the Senate Judiciary Committee,* Estes Kefauver, chairman (January 28–May 6, 1958, 85th Congress, 1st session); *Motor Vehicle Safety, Hearings before the House Subcommittee on Health and Safety of the Interstate and Foreign Commerce Committee,* Kenneth Roberts, chairman (July 7–9, 1959, 86th Congress, 1st session); *Automobile Seatbelt Standards, Hearings before the Subcommittee of the House Interstate and Foreign Commerce Committee,* Kenneth Roberts, chairman (August 17, 1962, 87th Congress, 2nd session); *Federal Role in Traffic Safety: Examination of Public and Private Agencies' Activities and the Role of the Federal Government, Senate Committee on Government Operations,* Abraham Ribicoff, chairman (March 22, 1965–March 22, 1966, 89th Congress, 1st session).

Among important government-published technical reports are *Radiological Health Data* (Division of Radiological Health, Public Health Service, Washington, D.C.) and *Public Health Reports* (Health Services and Mental Health Administration, Rockville, Md.). *The Surgeon General's Report on Smoking and Health* (Office of the Surgeon General, Public Health Service) presented the most complete review of evidence about the health consequences of smoking available in 1964. Subsequent reports have brought that review up to date. Judicial decisions relevant to the case studies were found in *Supreme Court Reports* and regional court reports (West Publications, St. Paul, Minn.). State legislative hearings included those of the California State Legislature, Joint Fact Finding Committee, "Un-American Activities in California," Jack B. Tenney, chairman (Sacramento, Calif., 1943, on file, CSCM), and reports of the New York State Legislature, *Motor Vehicles and Traffic and Highway Safety* (Albany, Legislative Document Series, 1961–1963).

The monthly *Consumer Reports* (1963–1980) and *Consumers' Research Bulletin* (1928–1980) provided essential outlets for consumer criticism. Also of use for the period since 1967 was the *Journal of Consumer Affairs*, published by the American Council on Consumer Interests. Other consumer periodicals useful for background information included *Bread and Butter* (1941–1945), *The Bulletin of the St. Louis Better Business Bureau* (1940–1947), *The Consumer* (1935–1937); *Consumer Information Service Bulletin* (1939–1941), *Consumers on the March* (various titles, 1945–1954), *American Home Economics Association Education Service* (1943–1948), and *Consumer Clearinghouse Newsletter* (1941–1943).

Publications of credit unions, the cooperative movement, and the labor movement often supported consumer causes. Among others, I consulted *Eastern States Cooperator* (1937–1940), *Consumers Defender* (1935–1942), and the syndicated consumer affairs column "Advice to Consumers" published in AFL-CIO publications, including the *Railway Carmen's Journal* and *The Postal Transport Journal*.

During the period following World War II, scientific publications—including *Science, Science Newsletter, Scientific American,* and the *Bulletin of Atomic Scientists*—considered the social and environmental consequences of scientific and technological developments. Beginning in the late 1920s, business and advertising magazines—especially *Business Week, Printer's Ink, Tide, Advertising Age,* and *Fortune*—kept watch on the activities of consumer groups, as did the newspapers *New York Times* and *Wall Street Journal*. Trade journals and industry reports reflected the attitudes of businesses criticized by consumer groups; among those were reports of the Tobacco Industry Research Council, *Automotive Industries* magazine, and the *National Dairy Council Newsletter*.

Reader's Digest, as the text of this book indicated, occupied a unique place in popularizing the need for greater concern about the dangers of both driving and smoking. Among journals of politics and letters discussing those and other consumer problems, the ones I turned to often were: *The New Republic* (1914–1964), *The Nation* (1927–1964), *Survey Graphic* (1921–1964), *Common Sense* (1932–1946), *The Reporter* (1949–1964), *The Atlantic* (1946–1964), *Harper's* (1946–1964), and *The New Yorker* (1945–1964). Women's magazines contained consumer advice as a journalistic staple; *Good Housekeeping* (1885–1964) and *Women's Home Companion* (1896–1957) were representative. During the period of this study, the mass newsweeklies *Time, Newsweek, Life,* and *Look,* and also television and radio commentaries brought consumer protest to national attention after the topics had been discussed elsewhere and in greater detail.

Transcripts of tape-recorded oral-history memoirs and conversations, housed at CSCM, helped me to understand better the personal experiences and attitudes of consumer activists. Varying restrictions were placed upon the access to interviews; those that I found valuable were cited at appropriate points in the notes and text. During the course of my research and as an interviewer for the oral-history program of CSCM, I was fortunate to speak with Colston Warne, Caroline Ware, Stuart Chase, Irving Michelson, Edward Brecher, Fred Wood, Joseph Ulman, Dr. Harold Aaron, William Pabst, Boris Tourin, Warren Brarren, Monti Florman, Mark and Helen Starr, Peter Schuck, Lowell Dodge, Clarence Ditlow, Wallace Janssen, George Robertson, and Charles Weaver. I examined the oral-history memoirs of Rexford G. Tugwell and Paul Douglas within the Herbert H. Lehman project at the Oral History Collection of Columbia University. I received helpful correspondence from Ralph Nader, Dexter Masters, and Mary C. Phillips, the wife and collaborator of F. J. Schlink.

The most informative of the published autobiographical works that I used were Maud Nathan, *The Story of an Epoch-Making Movement* (New York: Doubleday, Page and Co., 1926), an account of the work of the National Consumers League; Dr. Harvey Wiley, *The History of the Crime Against the Food and Drug Law* (Washington, D.C.: privately published, 1929), a description of Wiley's efforts to procure an effective law and his subsequent disillusionment with federal enforcement; and Paul Douglas, *In the Fullness of Time* (New York: Harcourt Brace Jovanovich, 1972), a portrait that included some discussion of consumer activities.

Writers who contributed to my understanding of the development of consumer protest were noted in chapter 1. Among the most penetrating and perhaps the most influential insights about the social contours of consumption in America were those of Thorstein Veblen, especially *The Theory of the Leisure Class* (New York: A. M. Kelley, 1899); *Absentee*

Ownership: The Case of America (New York: B. W. Huebsch, 1923); and *The Theory of Business Enterprise* (New York: Charles Scribner's Sons, 1904). John Diggins, *The Bard of Savagery: Thorstein Veblen and Modern Social Theory* (New York: Seabury Press, 1978), offered a recent, original interpretation of Veblen's relationship to Marx, Weber, and the sociological tradition. From more than two dozen books by Stuart Chase I found *The Tragedy of Waste* (New York: Macmillan, 1925), *Your Money's Worth* (New York: Macmillan, 1927), and *The Economy of Abundance* (New York: Macmillan, 1934) especially valuable.

Useful for indicating the development of ideas about consumer representation and rights were Hazyl Kyrk, *A Theory of Consumption* (Boston: Houghton Mifflin, 1923); Helen Sorenson, *The Consumer Movement* (New York: Harper and Brothers, 1941); and Persia Campbell, *Consumer Representation in the New Deal* (New York: Columbia University Press, 1940). Necessary for an understanding of consumer controversies of the 1930s were special issues of *Annals of the American Academy of Arts and Sciences*, CLXXXII, May 1928; CLXXXVIII, May 1934; and CXCII, March 1938.

Dissertations about consumer affairs generally explored questions related to marketing or home economics and reviewed historical issues peripherally. Notable exceptions were Lucy Black Creighton, "The Consumer Movement in the United States" (Harvard University, Ph.D. thesis in economics, 1968); Eugene Beem, "Consumer Rating and Testing Agencies in the United States" (University of Pennsylvania, Ph.D. thesis in business, 1951); and Sylvia Lane, "A Study of Selected Agencies that Evaluate Consumer Goods Qualitatively in the United States" (University of Southern California, Ph.D. thesis, 1957). Concerning the development of advertising, I consulted Daniel Andrew Pope, "The Emergence of National Advertising" (Columbia University, Ph.D. thesis, 1973). My work on the internal history of Consumers Union and Consumers' Research benefited from Sybil Schwartz Shainwald, "The Genesis and Growth of the First Consumer Product Testing Organization" (Columbia University, Master's thesis, 1971), Norman Katz, "Consumers Union: The Movement and the Magazine, 1936–1957," (Rutgers University, Ph.D. thesis, 1977), and Peter Samson, "The Emergence of a Consumer Interest in America" (University of Chicago, Ph.D. thesis, 1980).

Useful scholarly research that I consulted for the case studies in this book were: (smoking) Joseph C. Robert, *The Story of Tobacco in America* (New York: Knopf, 1949), Robert K. Heimann, *Tobacco and Americans* (New York: McGraw-Hill, 1960), and Lee Fritschler, *Smoking and Politics* (New York: Appleton-Century-Crofts, 1969); (fallout) Lawrence Wittner, *Rebels Against War: The American Peace Movement, 1941–1960*

(New York: Columbia University Press, 1969), Harold Karan Jacobson and Eric Stein, *Diplomats, Scientists and Politicians: The U.S. and the Nuclear Test Ban Negotiations* (Ann Arbor: University of Michigan Press, 1966), Robert A. Divine, *Blowing on the Wind* (New York: Oxford University Press, 1978); (automotive safety) William Haddon, Edward Suchman, and David Klein (eds.), *Accident Research: Methods and Approaches* (New York: Harper and Row, 1964), John Rae, *The American Automobile* (Chicago: University of Chicago Press, 1965), and James J. Flink, *The Car Culture* (Cambridge, Mass.: MIT Press, 1975). Two important discussions of the effect of organized consumer protest on the passage of food and drug legislation were Oscar Anderson, *The Health of a Nation: Harvey W. Wiley and the Fight for Pure Food* (Chicago: University of Chicago Press, 1958) and Charles O. Jackson, *Food and Drug Legislation in the New Deal* (Princeton: Princeton University Press, 1970). The best review of consumer challenges to the advertising profession was Otis Pease, *The Responsibilities of American Advertising* (New Haven, Yale University Press, 1959). Concerning the work of Ralph Nader and the consumer movement of the mid and late 1960s, one starting point was William T. Kelley (ed.), *The New Consumerism: Selected Readings* (Columbus, Ohio: Grid, Inc., 1973). Charles McCarry, *Citizen Nader* (New York: New American Library, 1972) presented a critical but close analysis of Nader's early work. Mark Nadel, *The Politics of Consumer Protection* (Indianapolis: Bobbs-Merrill, 1971) offered an interesting view of the passage of consumer legislation of the 1960s.

Organized consumer protest has received less attention from historians than it warrants. Understandably, there has been greater interest in the emergence of the American consumer culture. David Potter, *People of Plenty: Economic Abundance and the American Character* (Chicago: University of Chicago Press, 1954) was and is still an excellent introduction to the problem. The work of John Kenneth Galbraith, beginning with *American Capitalism: A Theory of Countervailing Power* (Boston: Houghton Mifflin, 1952), related the development of aggressive and insatiable consumerism to the imperatives of corporations. Recent investigations of interest included Allis R. Wolfe, *Persia Campbell* (New York: Consumers Union Foundation, 1981), a portrait of a leading consumer advocate; Ann Douglas, *The Feminization of American Culture* (New York: Knopf, 1976), which locates the roots of twentieth-century popular consumerism in the reorientation of the nineteenth-century literary marketplace; Stewart Ewen, *Captains of Consciousness: Advertising and the Social Roots of the Consumer Culture* (New York; McGraw-Hill, 1977), which attributes the success of modern capitalists to the manipulative effects of advertising; and an interesting recent work by Richard Fox,

Jackson Lears, Robert Westbrook, et al., *The Therapeutic Roots of the Consumer Culture* (New York: Pantheon Press, 1983). Daniel Boorstin in *The Americans, The Democratic Experiment* (New York, 1973) and in other works presented the diversity of consumption in America as a material expression of democratic ideals. There is no full treatment on the special role of women in consumer organizations, but feminist scholarship has considered questions related to consumer resistance. See, for example, Delores Hayden, *A Grand Domestic Revolution, Feminists' Revolt Against the American Home* (Cambridge, Mass: MIT Press, 1980) and Barbara Ehrenreich and Deidre English, *For Her Own Good: 150 Years of Experts' Advice to Women* (Garden City, New York: Anchor Press, 1978). Pertinent to understanding the political context of consumerism in the decades since World War II was John Morton Blum, *V Was for Victory: Culture and Politics in Wartime America* (New York and San Diego: Harcourt Brace Jovanovich, 1976), which connects government procurement policies as well as domestic prosperity during World War II to the emergence of a postwar consumer culture dominated by a few hundred large corporations.

Index